BILLY MARTIN

Sports Books by Gene Schoor

FOOTBALL'S GREATEST COACH, VINCE LOMBARDI
THE STORY OF YOGI BERRA
BART STARR: A BIOGRAPHY
BABE DIDRIKSON—THE WORLD'S GREATEST WOMAN ATHLETE
JOE DIMAGGIO: A BIOGRAPHY

BILLY MARTIN

Gene Schoor

DOUBLEDAY & COMPANY, INC., GARDEN CITY, NEW YORK
1980

For photographs in this book the author wishes to acknowledge
his indebtedness to . . .
Newsworld Photo Syndicate
The Daily News
New York Yankees
Wide World Photos
Associated Press Photos

Library of Congress Cataloging in Publication Data

Schoor, Gene.
    Billy Martin.

    1. Martin, Alfred Manuel, 1928– 2. Baseball
managers—United States—Biography. I. Title.
GV865.M35S36   796.357'0924 [B]
ISBN: 0-385-15280-9
Library of Congress Catalog Card Number 79-7699

In addition to the numerous baseball people who spoke with me about Billy Martin, including Billy Martin, I have drawn on the works of numerous sportswriters who have written about Martin over the past three decades of his baseball life.

My sincere gratitude to the following:

Irv Goodman, Roger Kahn, Dick Schaap, Ed Linn for articles in *Sport* magazine. Robert Creamer, Ron Fimrite, Frank Deford of *Sports Illustrated*. Red Smith, Dave Anderson, Arthur Daley, Murray Chass in the New York *Times*. Milt Gross, Jimmy Cannon in the New York *Post*. Sports Editor Dick Young, Phil Pepe, Bill Verigan in the New York *Daily News*.

Mickey Mantle for his book *The Quality of Courage*

Peter Golenbock for his fine book *Dynasty*

Dave Anderson for his outstanding book *The Yankees*

Norman Smith for his book *Return of Billy the Kid*

Whitey and Mickey, by Joe Durso

Thurman Munson, by Marty Appell

The Bronx Zoo, by Sparky Lyle and Peter Golenbock

Baseball As I Have Known It, by Fred Lieb

The Best Team That Money Could Buy, by Steve Jacobson

And to friend and voice of the Yankees, Mel Allen, and the entire Sports Department of the Minneapolis *Star* for their outstanding contribution.

CONTENTS

BILLY MARTIN

CHAPTER ONE

"The Little Bastard"

"HE'S A FEISTY LITTLE SON-OF-A-BITCH," SAID THE FORMER GEN-eral manager of the Cleveland Indians, Frank Lane. "He's the kind of guy you'd like to kill if he's playing for the other team, but you'd like ten of him on your own side. The little bastard."

The "little bastard" was Billy Martin, sometimes affection-ately known as Billy the Kid, a name he liked well enough to sew on a tab and attach at various times to his sunglasses, in-side his tailored cowboy shirts, jackets, or on his athletic sup-porters.

Casey Stengel, that Old Professor, loved the "little son-of-a-bitch."

"That fresh punk," he proclaimed loud and often enough, "how I love him. The freshest kid which ever played for me."

Joe DiMaggio, the great star and the most reserved of Yan-kee players, befriended Billy the first day the Kid appeared at spring training with the Yankees in 1950. He greeted Billy like a long-lost pal from his home in the San Francisco Bay Area. After the first practice, DiMaggio walked up to Martin who was with a group of other players and called out:

"Hey, Dago, let's go have some dinner."

"It practically shook up the whole clubhouse," Martin said. "And it really floored me."

"You had to be around the team for at least four or five years, and you had to be a star, before you could say any more than hello to DiMaggio," said Whitey Ford, "but Joe and Billy became instant friends, and it was DiMaggio who squired Billy around the big city; he brought him to Toots Shor's res-taurant, introduced Billy to the great man himself, and in a few days Billy became a well-known figure at the Shor AC."

"Joe knows class when he sees it," is the way Billy Martin explained the buddy relationship with the Yankee Clipper, "and seeing that I was an Italian from the San Francisco Bay Area, I guess that had something to do with it, and we got along just fine. I could even kid around with Joe and he got a big laugh," said Billy, and he flashed that shy, mischievous grin of his, a grin that was going to win him countless friends and enemies in baseball.

Billy roomed with Phil Rizzuto for a while, until Billy got tired of acting as Phil's messenger boy, delivering the popular Phil's telephone calls, handling his mail, and at the same time acting as his bodyguard.

Billy roomed with Mickey Mantle, and Mickey, along with Whitey Ford, were his closest pals. They were dubbed The Three Musketeers and pretty much lived up to the name with their zest for fun, their derring-do, and just plain mischief. They're still great friends. Mickey and Billy Martin are as close as two brothers can ever hope to be.

But there were many others, particularly in and around baseball, who felt less kindly disposed to Billy the Kid, and that's putting it mildly.

"You little bush bastard!" Johnny Mize spit at him in their first encounter.

Chicago Cubs pitcher Jim Brewer called him a "little Dago son-of-a-bitch," and the Kid promptly dropped him with a right to the chin.

It wasn't so much the "Dago" that irked the Kid. Joe DiMaggio, himself of Italian extraction, called Billy "Dago," but affectionately. And Billy called himself a Dago as often as not.

"I'm proud to be a Dago," he said, not as a challenge, but as a statement of fact.

It must have been the "son-of-a-bitch" that turned on the Kid, or maybe just the way Jim Brewer said it.

In any case, there was certainly no love lost between Brewer and Billy Martin.

Nor was there any love lost between Clint Courtney of the

St. Louis Browns and the Kid. They fought and tangled three times before Courtney recognized the better man.

Billy handed Red Sox outfielder Jimmy Piersall a beating under the Stadium stands. He battered huge Dave Boswell, who was pitching for him when he was managing the Minnesota Twins. He did the same to Howard Fox, traveling secretary for the Twins, in the lobby of a hotel.

Larry Gura, Elliott Maddox, Reggie Jackson, and a host of ballplayers, managers, coaches, umpires, just fans, and an entire corps of sportswriters, who never got to challenge the Kid to a brawl, would rather chew their spit than say anything approaching a good word for the "little bastard."

No one could claim an indifference to Martin. He was loved or hated. There was nothing in between.

The fans booed him or cheered him, but love or hate they jammed the ball parks to see him in action, with his glove, with his bat, with his brawling mouth, and with his accurate two-fisted punching, or with all of them at once. Later, when he had put away his bat and hung up his glove to coach and manage, the same fans, and more, crowded the parks to cheer the underdog teams at Minneapolis, Detroit, Texas, and the Yankees that Billy Martin fired up into contenders, pennant winners, and world champions.

For certain, most fans loved Billy the Kid a bit less than they hated him but, when the chips were down in a battle between the Kid and the front office, which happened often enough, the majority of baseball fans were loud in his support, and they let the top brass and the newspapers know it.

As for the top brass, the love between management and the Kid was always something less than skin deep. Billy Martin was too willful and stubborn and independent for the front office. Club owners hired him because they needed him. And once they had him, he delivered a fighting, scrapping ball club that challenged the leaders consistently and brought out the fans.

Club owners had him on the carpet regularly, they read the riot act to him, they threatened him, fined him, fired him, but

Billy Martin never backed away from any club owner. He simply never learned how to kiss anyone's boots, and he certainly was never afraid of anything or anyone.

Club owners were delighted to sign Billy to a contract, but once they had him, they didn't know how to handle him. They couldn't stand his honesty and his guts, but with their thoughts always on the gate receipts, they loved the action and excitement he brought them.

Sometimes a ballplayer's temperament gets all the publicity, and his ability as a player or manager merits little notice in the sports columns because of it. Billy Martin was never considered a superstar, neither by most ballplayers nor most sportswriters. "Average" was the best they ever said of him.

But Casey Stengel thought Billy Martin was an outstanding player, and the Old Professor knew more baseball than many of the so-called experts who played or wrote about the game, as most sportswriters will readily admit. And old Case was right about Billy the Kid.

The Kid was a battler. As a player he went after every ball hit within his area. He was a leader, a spirited, go-get-'em ballplayer, who placed team loyalty and love for his teammates above anything else.

His lifetime batting average was a meager .257, but he was a clutch hitter. He made that one hit in four times at bat count. When the chips were down, Martin delivered.

He saved a World Series for the Yankees with an almost impossible catch of a wind-driven, lost-in-the-sun, sky-high pop fly in 1952 and was the batting star of the Yankees during the Series, hitting well over .350.

The Kid drove himself. He never knew the word "quit." He was a winner. He had to be a winner. He took losing hard, hard enough to sit down in the locker room and let the tears run down his face, unashamedly.

Player, coach, or manager, his attitude toward the game was always the same. He gave everything to the game. He had to win. And he expected everyone who played with him, or for him, to have the same attitude, to give the game everything he had, to win.

He could forgive errors in the field. He could even forgive one of his players, when he was managing the ball club, if he missed a signal: bunt, take, hit-and-run. To err is human. But if a player took it easy, failed to hustle on a play, or showed little team spirit, Billy Martin would neither forgive nor forget. For certain the man would get a loud earful he'd remember for a long time. And if he didn't take the lead out of his feet, he wasn't going to last for very long on Mr. Billy Martin's roster.

"A feisty little son-of-a-bitch . . . the little bastard."

Quick with his biting sarcasm, quicker with his fists, pugnacious, cocky, brash, the chip always light on his shoulders, right from the beginning, Billy the Kid was all of that. But there was something more to the man below the surface that hardly ever made the sports pages, because it wasn't "good copy." On the field away from baseball there was a completely different Billy Martin, a Billy Martin with an amazing, intelligent interest in the history and background of the Civil War, a collector of Civil War books, and with an almost professorial knowledge of the causes underlying the great conflict between the states. A Billy Martin who was a shy, honest human being with a generous respect for the truth, loyalty, courage, and, yes, that old-fashioned faith in the Church, Jesus Christ, and the Almighty.

There were headlines plenty in print when Billy Martin, perhaps undiplomatically but honestly, publicly blasted a player for not hustling, or the front office, for not supporting him with the proper trades, but scarcely a word, if any, about Billy the Kid attending Mass in St. Patrick's Cathedral every Sunday morning when the Yankees were at home. Cardinal Spellman knew him well. Cardinal Cooke knows him well, too. The Kid has carried a picture of St. Jude in his pockets almost as long as he can remember. St. Jude is his patron saint. He wears a gold cross, always, pinned on his baseball cap.

If Billy Martin says, "Jesus Christ took a whip to the money changers in the Temple," to explain, not to apologize for, his own quick temper, "and that's not a bad guy to follow," he doesn't ask the Lord for any favors. Particularly, he doesn't ask Him for any favors on the diamond.

"God decides who wins and who loses," Billy says, and he profoundly believes it. "Everything is in God's hands."

And after a moment he will add, "You know, there are lots of good Catholics on the other clubs, too."

For all the advertised ego of the man, there is a streak of humility, decency, loyalty, and love that surprises everyone but his closest friends.

His friends and the people around him know his courage, too, his moral as well as his physical courage.

There was the day in Boston when Phil Rizzuto got a letter from some lunatic Red Sox fan, threatening to shoot to kill him the next time he played in Fenway Park.

Phil was naturally tense dressing up for the game that afternoon. So was Casey and all of the Yankees.

"Let's change uniforms," said Martin. "You wear my shirt. I'll wear yours."

Rizzuto looked at Casey, and old Case shrugged his shoulders.

"Come on," pressed the Kid. "I'll wear your No. 10. You wear my No. 1. I'll take the chance. Be the target. Anyways, I can run faster than you can," said Billy with a smile.

And that's the way they took the field, Martin wearing Rizzuto's No. 10 on his back, ready to take the bullet of the crazed Red Sox fan.

Billy the Kid did a lot of moving on the diamond that afternoon. He wasn't about to make himself an easy target for the gunman. Fortunately, however, the man with the gun was apparently not in the park, and there was no shooting. Phil, after the chorus of boos that greeted him for the No. 1 he wore on his shirt, was glad to get back into his own uniform. But how about that Billy Martin? Was it just his guts that dared the bullet? Or was it the profound sense of loyalty and friendship that so very few who followed his career were able to really appreciate?

It was the Kid's sense of loyalty that tore him apart from the one man he had really learned to love, the Old Professor, Casey Stengel. Casey, the Kid felt, had been disloyal to him when Billy was traded away from the Yankees, and for years he wouldn't speak to him.

He could write an article about the old skipper and title it "I Loved the Old Man," but, much as Casey tried to bridge the gap between them, Billy Martin wouldn't say boo to the Old Man.

"I guess I was the proudest Yankee of them all," said the Kid. "I don't mean a false pride. I mean a deep love-pride."

Even after he had been traded from the Yankees, in what he considered a raw deal, it took the Kid years to get over his loyalty to the club, New York, and its players.

Martin was a throwback to the swashbuckling days of sworn, blood friendship, or farther back to the blood fealties of the ancient tribes.

It was loyalty, and love, that gave Billy some of his most difficult times. When the hometown girl he had married wanted out of the marriage, her rejection of his loyalty and love nearly killed him. Rejection was tolerable, if it came from a man. The Kid had a built-in response for that kind of rejection: the old gesture with the thumb or a quick straight right to the jaw. But a woman, and the woman he loved; that he couldn't take.

He couldn't eat. He couldn't sleep. He practically lived on tranquilizers.

"I was about ready for a straitjacket," said the Kid.

Martin has been called a male chauvinist, and perhaps with some justice. He vetoed an attempt to organize a players' wives' club, when he was managing the Twins, and he doesn't take kindly to female sportswriters visiting the locker room. He thinks that sort of thing doesn't do much for the morale of the club. Still, his love for women borders on adoration. And this holds true particularly for the second woman to become Mrs. Billy Martin.

This second marriage for the Kid was a lucky and happy one. He worships his exceedingly pretty Gretchen, an ex-airline stewardess, and the son she gave him, Billy Joe, is the apple of his eye.

Yes, Billy Martin has a flip side, a rich, warm, loving, sentimental, religious side to go with the rough, tough, cocky, belligerent Billy the Kid. How do you explain it?

How much of Billy Martin came with the genes he inherited? How much of him was fashioned by the poverty of his boyhood, the streets in which he grew up? Is he pugnacious to conceal some hard-riding inner fears? Is his need to be a winner a reaction to an inferiority complex? Is he rough and tough and quick with his fists to hide the sensitivities of a genuine sentimentalist?

Psychologists, psychiatrists, sociologists, and social-service workers would have a field day, dissecting and explaining the complicated character of the complicated Billy the Kid. But Billy shrugs them all off.

"I'm not interested in anyone knowing the real Billy Martin," he says. "I don't care if no one knows the real me—that is, no one but Jesus Christ."

CHAPTER TWO

Alfred Manuel Martin

BILLY MARTIN NEVER KNEW EITHER OF HIS GRANDFATHERS. He didn't even know his own father until he was about fourteen years old. Let the psychologists make the most of it.

His maternal grandfather, Nicholas Salvini, was an Italian fisherman who, like so many other Italian fishermen, left his homeland for the lush fishing grounds of the San Francisco Bay Area. He settled in West Berkeley, in a poor working-class district around the Bay and, at the age of thirty-five, sent to Italy for a postcard bride.

The bride was still in her teens, a mere girl. She took one look at her prospective husband, who was almost as old as her father and already bald, and she began to sob.

"I don't want to marry that old man," she cried, in Italian of course; she never learned to speak English.

But marry him she did, and she fell in love with him, too. "Old" Nicholas Salvini was away from home for months, often as long as six months, on one fishing boat or another, up toward Alaska or west toward the China coast but, as their tiny but pretty daughter Joan remembers well, he came home always to a great loving welcome, and celebration. The Stars and Stripes were run up on a flagpole of their wood-frame, two-story little house, and Salvini's daughter Joan was sent by ferry to San Francisco to pick up two gallons of whiskey, at $1.50 a gallon, at Martinelli's.

"Papa liked whiskey for breakfast."

Papa also loved his family. He'd come home from his long fishing trips with $200 or $300 in his pockets, much of it in silver; and he delighted in throwing it all over the house.

"This is for you, and this is for you!"

It made a man feel good to know that he was providing well for his family. It was a happy family.

Joan, following in her mother's footsteps, married early. She was only sixteen years old when she became Mrs. Pesano, and not much older when she gave birth to her first son, Frank.

But the marriage didn't last and very quickly she became a divorcee.

Then came Alfred Martin, a Portuguese fisherman out of the Island of Maui in the Hawaiians. He was a big fellow, maybe six-two, and tough. On Maui, they called him the toughest son-of-a-gun on the island. In the Bay Area, he was known as the Por-to-gee, and fully respected for his brawn.

He was a hard man to resist, and Joan married again, though she knew from the beginning that the marriage was a mistake.

"Let's face it," she says. "We just didn't get along."

They managed to stay together for a while, however, long enough for Joan Martin to give birth to her second son.

"He was late in coming," she says. "He was a ten-month baby. I thought I'd never have him."

But she did.

One fine day she was hanging out the laundry to dry and fell, right into a coal bin.

She got herself some pretty bad bruises but, the next day, May 16, 1928, she was delivered of her second baby.

"Right in the room he uses now," she says, "whenever he gets home."

She named the baby Alfred Manuel, after his father, but even a son wasn't enough to keep that ill-starred marriage together.

Alfred Manuel, Jr., was just about eight months old when his unhappy father walked out of the house, never to return.

The first time Billy actually met his father, he was fourteen years old and was the star of his junior high school baseball team. He didn't see him again for another five years until he was playing ball for the Triple-A Oakland Oaks. They've met since, even had long talks together, but the emotional father-son, son-father relationship never developed between them, never even got started.

Though he retained the name Martin, Billy feels much closer to Jack Downing, his mother's third husband. Jack Downing was Irish-Canadian, and he was essentially a kind and gentle sort of man. He treated Billy much as he did his own children.

Downing was a hard worker but jobs were scarce and pay was low in the Depression years. There was never enough money to make ends meet in the Downing house. Still, young Billy never felt the pinch. Everybody in the neighborhood was poor and nobody knows what poverty really means when everyone around him is in the identical situation.

Besides, Billy had his grandmother living next door and her love made up for anything he might have thought he missed.

Actually, when Billy's mother married for the third time, he went to live with his grandmother Salvini. She lived right next door in an identical two-story wooden frame house.

The relationship between grandson and grandma was very close. They actually slept in the one bed until Billy was thirteen, and his kicking in his sleep disturbed the old lady, so she bought him a small bed of his own.

It was Grandmother Salvini who gave him the name Billy. She called him "Bello," Italian for cute, or pretty. The "Bello" became "Billy" with the kids in the street, with the rest of the family. It wasn't until he got to school that Billy learned that his name was Alfred Manuel.

"My grandmother," says Billy now, reminiscing about his earliest years, "used to bite my hand whenever she thought I'd done something wrong. If I sneaked into the house late at night, which I used to do every now and then, she'd bang me on the back of the head and I'd have to say my prayers in Italian, so she'd be sure I was saying the right words, before I went to bed."

It was always with love, of course, and strange for an old lady who never really became Americanized, she encouraged Billy to become a baseball player.

That was one area in which he needed little if any encouragement.

At Berkeley High School, he was not a good student. He even got an F in physical education.

"That phys-ed teacher," Billy will recall with a bit of a grin, "had the courage to ask me for a couple of World Series tickets, when I was playing for the Yankees; and I got them for him.

"No, I wasn't much of a student," adds Billy, "but I did play some baseball, basketball, and even football.

"The only teacher I ever had," says Billy with a wry grin, "who took an interest in me was my English teacher. She gave us books to read but I didn't read them. One day she gave me a book on Lou Gehrig. I read that. She asked me some questions about the book and I practically told her the entire story. She gave me a good mark."

He was a .400-plus hitter on the school baseball team. He was a star on its football squad. As a forward in basketball, he set a school record with an average of 15.6 points a game, and he even won a basketball scholarship to Santa Clara University, which he turned down because it was baseball he wanted to play.

"I knew I was good," he will add, "but I couldn't get rid of those doubts.

"But when I got on the field with the other guys, I would say to myself, 'Am I?'

"I was sure I was. I knew deep down I was. But I had to prove it to myself and I couldn't let on how I felt. I had to be sure. I had to be cocky smart. All the time I knew I was good. . . ."

Billy shrugged and grinned again. "It sounds a little confused," he said. "I know I can do it. . . . I don't know whether I can or not. . . . Then I get out there and prove to all of them I can. I'm cocky. I pop off. They say I'm fresh."

Maybe it was the doubting and frustrations that got him into so many fights. Maybe it was the ridicule he would have to take constantly: about the size of his nose, which was indeed large, or about his jug ears.

"Hey, Big Nose!"

"Pinocchio!"

"Banana Nose!"

He was short for his age, and skinny, but whoever thought they could get away taunting him because of his size and weight were quickly disabused.

"I didn't care how big they were, or how much they weighed," says Martin. "I went after them. And I had a punch!"

And there were many who could attest to that punch.

He took on a Golden Gloves winner and knocked him out with a right to the jaw. He was suspended from the school baseball team for knocking out the Heywood High School pitcher during a ball game. When the heckling of a rival school crowd became too much for him, he whacked a ball directly into their section of the grandstand.

Fighting came as a natural way of living for a kid who was brought up on the streets.

"My childhood was different," Billy said with a shy grin. "I grew up in a very tough neighborhood in Berkeley where you either had to fight or run. I learned a lot about life as a kid on the streets. Guys learn it now when they're twenty-five. You had to fight, fight, fight, and win to survive. Every day there'd be a new guy who called you a name and challenged you to a fight. Fifty to a hundred kids would be sitting in a circle in Jenkton Park, and you came along, and a new guy came along and challenged you. They did it to everybody. That's just the way they lived. It was like a jungle. I used to watch a lot of pro boxers train for their fights, and I would copy the way they held their hands, and then I would practice my punches on a punching bag. And in time I became pretty good, and I whipped a lot of kids on the street. And after you beat up a lot of guys," said Billy, "they leave you alone."

Actually, no one had to bait Billy into a scrap. His temper

was too short for that. Let someone cast a slur on a friend and he was there ready with his fists to make the culprit pay for his lip. He wasn't more than a skinny, little eleven-year-old kid when he turned to take on a crowd of grown men for just whistling at his mother.

"I really got mad and wanted to fight those guys," says Billy.

Fortunately, his mother restrained the young Sir Galahad.

"What's wrong with whistling?" she demanded. "They just like what they see. And don't you ever forget," she added, "your mamma has the prettiest little fanny in town."

At eleven, he would have gotten his butt kicked around by his mother's whistling admirers, but Billy was afraid of nobody, no matter the weight, age, or size. And he was a good scrapper, as anybody who tested his ability with his fists will testify. He could punch and he had fast hands. He was so good and proficient a scrapper that a lot of his peers were sure Billy would wind up as a professional fighter.

One of his pals was a professional fighter, Dick Foster, who fought against Young Corbett III and other good boxers, and Billy Martin was around to see most of Foster's fights. But the ring never really excited the Kid.

"I fought only when I had to," he says, which was often enough.

Right from the beginning it was baseball with Billy, and nothing would lure him away from it, not even that basketball scholarship to Santa Clara.

Father Moore was a wise, perceptive, and sensitive man of the cloth.

"When Billy went into professional baseball," he said, "I prayed for him.

"Life had made him vulnerable," added the good Father. "I prayed he would get wise counseling."

It was to the same Father Moore that Billy Martin gave the Cadillac he got along with his MVP award.

But the church was not the only place Billy Martin worked to bring in that extra cash his family needed so badly. After school, and summers too, he worked as equipment manager at a playground, carried mail for the post office, was a packer in a Heinz plant, and worked in a steel mill.

Early on, Billy Martin gave evidence of his sense of responsibility, to himself and perhaps even more to the team. It was a trait that never left him but rather grew and matured with the years, particularly on the diamond.

Billy Martin's life has been a difficult one, and rather than retreat and give up, he chose instead to fight for his self-respect and a cause he deemed important to him. To that end Billy is still fighting, because his doubts and frustrations are deeply rooted within, and his fears of poverty and rejection still lurk just below the surface.

CHAPTER THREE

Casey

BILLY MARTIN WAS PLAYING SEMIPRO BALL WHEN HE WAS STILL in high school, on the sandlot they called James Kinney Playfield.

During the off-season, professional stars and college baseball players would regularly collect on Saturday and Sunday afternoons, looking for a pick-up game. There were ex-big-leaguers like Cookie Lavagetto and Augie Galan, and a young college All-American football star named Jackie Jensen, who came from Berkeley. There were players from the Triple-A Pacific Coast League Oakland Oaks. There were minor-league players with years of experience, in their twenties and thirties. And there was Billy Martin, fifteen years of age, a sandwich consisting of half a loaf of bread stuffed with salami, pushed in his pocket.

The usual flip of the coin, and the men would choose up sides, and Billy would find himself on one team or the other. It didn't take him long to prove that as a teen-ager he could play along with the men who were much older, more experienced, perhaps stronger than he was.

He would have liked to play the infield, second, shortstop, third, but generally they shoved him into the outfield, where he would take a bite out of his oversized salami sandwich between outs. Occasionally, however, he did get to play second or short, and he'd have to forget the sandwich. He'd rather play ball than eat anytime.

His skillful and aggressive play didn't go unnoticed among the professional ballplayers. He caught the eye of Augie Galan, who had played in the major leagues for sixteen years with the Cubs, the Dodgers, and the Reds. Galan, who was born and

brought up in Berkeley and was Martin's boyhood idol, was
particularly impressed with Billy.

"He's kind of rough around the edges," Galan said to Red
Adams, who managed a team called the Junior Oaks that performed before the professional games at the Oakland ball
park, "and I don't know how much real ability Martin's got,
but you have to stop and admire the way he hustles, and his
spirit is all gung-ho. And he's a smart-ass kid, always pumping
me for information about certain plays. He's chattering all the
time, never stops talking baseball."

Red Adams carefully looked Billy over, and invited him to
join the team. And as a member of the Oaks, Billy soon became one of the leading players of the club.

"How would you like to work out and practice with Oakland?" he asked Martin, and Billy, all emotion, was too
choked up to speak. He just nodded.

Adams put Billy into the Oaks' lineup, during the pregame
practice period.

"How do you like that kid at short?" he asked the manager
of the Acorns as they watched the practice drills.

The Oaks had a new manager that year—Casey Stengel,
whose career had hit a new low at fifty-eight years of age, seemingly on the way down after a big-league career that began in
Brooklyn in 1912 and now in 1948 was back in the minor
leagues.

Chances are that no one ever had more fun playing baseball
than Charles Dillon Stengel, and while he had experienced all
the woes with which managers are afflicted from time to time,
he could look back on the overall picture and say that it had
been a marvelous life.

He was born in Kansas City (hence the nickname, derived
from K.C.) on July 30, 1890, and ripened into first a dental
student and then a cab driver in his late youth. The career
being formed at Western Dental College did not pan out, apparently because Stengel found it difficult as a left-hander to
handle right-handed dental instruments. As a player, he was
discovered in 1911 by Larry Sutton, the Dodgers' famous one-

man scouting staff, and in view of Stengel's subsequent career, with its lights, its shadows, and its laughs, it was fitting and proper that the discovery should have been accidental. Sutton, who had no specific assignments from the front office, but roamed the country at will, went to Aurora, Illinois, for the simple reason that he had never been there and wanted to see what it looked like. Gravitating naturally to the ball park, he saw Stengel, whom he had not heard of but whom he was quick to appraise as almost a major-league outfielder although, as he was to learn, Casey had had only one season as a professional, divided between Kankakee in the Northern Association and Maysville in the Blue Grass League. On his recommendation, the Dodgers bought Casey, farmed him out to Montgomery in the Southern League in 1912 and, in August of that season, ordered him to report to Brooklyn.

"I was full of fire and vinegar at Maysville," Casey recalled several years ago, "and I practiced sliding into third base on my way to and from the outfield every inning. There was a lunatic asylum behind center field and the people out there used to applaud my slides more than home runs. They must have recognized a kindred soul."

Stengel reported to Brooklyn and in his first game with the Dodgers drove out four straight hits. The next day, in a preview of many such episodes, Casey slid spikes high into the Chicago Cubs' great Johnny Evers, guarding second base. Evers was outraged. "You do that one more time, busher," he screamed, "one more time like that, and you eat this." He shook the ball in Stengel's face. Stengel lying across the bag, looked up at Evers, and said, "Mister, I been sliding this way a long time and I don't figure to switch now. So if you're gonna make me eat that ball you better start. The next time I come down here I'll rip your legs apart, and don't you forget it."

Dodger fans immediately took to the smiling, swaggering tough kid. He could hit, run, and throw, and for all his good nature and clowning he could be as rough and tough as any player in the league. He played in Brooklyn for six years and went from there to Pittsburgh and Philadelphia and in 1921 to the New York Giants. He was so happy at returning to the big city that he didn't even bother to pack up his things. He caught the first train out for New York and sent back to Philadelphia for his clothes.

Casey spent two and a half years with John McGraw and the New York Giants, and although he had slowed down in ten years of pounding the major-league trails, McGraw liked him for his fighting spirit, guts, and hustle, and used him as much as possible. He hit .368 in 1922, .339 in 1923. The Giants won the league championship three times in the three years he was with them and met the Yankees three times in the World Series. The Giants won the Series in 1921 and 1922. His role in the Giants' futile World Series stand against the Yankees in 1923 now stands as a sports classic.

Casey hit .417 for the six games. After one homer, he thumbed his nose at the mighty Yankees. He rubbed it even deeper on his second. Casey drove a ball of the center-field fence, and he was off for first. As he neared second, a shoelace came loose, and he began to drag the shoe to keep it on his foot. To the huge crowd, conscious of Stengel's age and mileage, the effect was that of a drunken old man weaving around the bases. But he got all the way around. As Casey wobbled and puffed across home plate his fiancée, Edna, turned to her father and said proudly, "What do you think of my hero now, Pa?"

Pa took another look at Stengel, now staggering into the arms of his teammates. "I just hope," he said, "he lives until the wedding."

In the fall of 1923 he was traded to the Boston Braves. Judge Emil Fuchs, who owned the Braves, also owned the Worcester club of the Eastern League and sent Casey to Worcester in 1925 as president, manager, and player.

He managed the Toledo club for six years, winning the pennant in 1927. In 1932, Casey returned to the Dodgers as a coach and then was appointed manager of the Dodgers in 1934.

Fired in 1936, Casey was back in 1938 as manager of the Boston Braves, surely one of the worst teams in baseball. He managed the Braves until 1943, then quit to move back to California.

But he was not to stay there very long, for he was hired in 1944 to manage the Milwaukee Brewers and guided the Brewers to a pennant. Once again he was on the move, this time to Kansas City, where his K.C. team finished in seventh place. In 1948 Casey once again headed for California, this time to manage the Oakland Oaks in the Pacific Coast League.

It was a move at fifty-eight years of age that was to take Casey to the highest pinnacle of success in the game he loved, and a historic career with the Yankees and the New York Mets.

In Oakland, after all these long, empty, victoryless years, Casey found himself with solid, possibly championship material to manage, and in his first season he skillfully guided the Oaks into second place. He had promised club owner Brick Laws that he would give him a winner, and so Casey checked and double-checked every promising young prospect in the Oakland area. So when Red Adams kept after Casey about Billy Martin, kept insisting the Kid was a future star, Casey took a long look and another look at Martin's play.

Later on, Casey said, "I swear when I first laid eyes on that skinny, funny-looking kid, I looked and watched and the more I watched him, the more I saw myself as a fresh young ballplayer."

"Casey, I'm telling you that kid Martin at short is the best-looking prospect I've ever seen," insisted Red Adams.

"That second baseman looks good," said Casey.

"You're looking at the wrong kid," came back Red. "The best player on the field there is your shortstop."

"The skinny kid?" said Case. "The one in the old clothes?"

Billy had come to the park in his own uniform. It was tattered, torn, and did not fit. The sleeves flapped as he dashed out after a ground ball, and he looked like a scarecrow on the field.

"Forget the uniform," said Red. "Just look at the way he comes up with every ball hit in his area. He's a gem."

"Sure," said Casey, and he began to walk away.

"He'll be back tomorrow," yelled Red Adams after old Case. "Take a good look at him, will you?"

Billy was back in the ball park, as promised, and Casey took a good look. He did more. He had Martin take the field for an hour as Casey smashed ball after ball to him at short. "Casey would give me a funny look and whack—he'd drive one right at me," Martin said. "I'd catch it and give him the limp wrist and throw it back. I stopped every ball he hit to me.

"I guess he liked the way I hustled and scrambled for the ball," said Billy Martin later. "Even when I couldn't make a clean stop, I was sure to get in front of every one he hit to me. I didn't miss one."

Talking about that first encounter with Billy the Kid, Casey would say, "He was tough and sassy and rough, but he was a fighter. I saw in Billy myself as a young ball player. Yessir, I looked across the field and in that kid, I saw old Casey once again 'fighting for a place in the sun.'"

In time, Casey and Billy Martin became like father and son. Stengel himself had always been a tough, scrappy brawler, and he recognized and encouraged those traits in Martin. Stengel would pay Billy twenty-five dollars to get hit by a pitched ball. Stengel would encourage him to fight back and to back up his teammates in fights on the field. "He's got it here in the heart, where it counts," Stengel would often say of his protégé.

When Eddie Leishman, a scout for the New York Yankees, sent out an SOS for a ballplayer to replace someone who had been injured on the Idaho Falls club, the Yankees' farm team in the Class C Pioneer League, Red Adams didn't hesitate to recommend Billy Martin.

Red checked with Stengel, and Case was just as quick, promoting the kid to Leishman.

Leishman, the proficient scout, checked up on the recommendation. The kid was skinny. He looked like he didn't weigh more than 135 pounds. But he hit the ball well, stopped everything that was hit to him, and more than anything else, it was his tremendous enthusiasm for the game, his gung-ho, his drive, that impressed Leishman.

"How would you like to play for Idaho Falls?" he asked Billy.

Billy didn't know much about Idaho Falls.

"How about Oakland?" he asked. "I'd rather play there."

Always straightforward, always to the point, always brash, Billy Martin.

"You'll be signed by Oakland. You'll be owned by Oakland. But you'll play for Idaho Falls," said Leishman. "If you're good enough, Casey will be asking for you."

"That's good enough for me," said Billy.

He saw Brick Laws, the owner of the Oakland club. There was the contract to sign, an event that was to turn out a little less than routine for Billy.

"We'll give you two hundred dollars a month," said Laws.

"That's OK with me," said Billy.

Two hundred dollars a month was a small fortune for young Martin. It was big money those days for a slum kid. Besides, it wasn't the paycheck that interested Billy; it was his first professional baseball contract.

"We'll give you a three-hundred-dollar bonus," added Brick Laws, as if he were handing the Kid a huge bribe.

Billy hadn't expected a bonus. He was too surprised to say anything, just nodded his head and tried to conceal his great joy. He didn't even have the time to think of what he was going to do with all that money.

Everything was going well, and in good order. Then came the bombshell.

"One thing more," said Brick Laws, "there's this street gang you hang around with."

Billy felt something coming. His back stiffened.

"My friends, sir," he said.

"You'll have to give up those friends," said Brick Laws. "You'll have to stop seeing them."

"Why, sir?" asked Billy, still polite, but the tension building in his jaw.

"Baseball can't tolerate hoodlums," said Laws.

"Friends like that will get you in trouble and out of the game for sure, and in a hurry."

Billy Martin hesitated, but only for a moment.

"Sir," he said, "if I have to give up my friends to play ball for you, then I don't play ball for you. I'm not signing the contract."

Baseball was all that Billy Martin dreamed of, as long as he could remember. His sole ambition had been to become a professional ballplayer. Only one thing in life meant more to him: the sense of loyalty that was the bloodstream of his code of honor.

What a throwback, inherited, learned in the streets; or was it his gut feeling about his father's deserting him and his mother when he was no more than eight months old?

Whatever it was, Brick Laws didn't press the issue. Loyalty is a rare quality, and Brick respected it. And he couldn't help admiring the great pride and spirit of the young fellow, either.

"OK," said Laws, "you win. Those friends of yours aren't going to do you much good, but here," he added, handing Billy the Oakland contract, "sign it, and have your mother sign. You're not of legal age."

Billy cooled down.

"Thank you, sir."

He signed the contract.

Eighteen-year-old Billy Martin was a professional ballplayer. Idaho Falls!

Out of that three-hundred-dollar bonus he bought himself the first pair of new slacks he ever owned and a new suitcase, luxuries he had never been able to afford before, and he was off to the Pioneer League and a great if tempestuous career.

His grandmother had always said he would become a baseball player. Billy always knew down deep he would become a ballplayer. What he didn't know, or even think about, then, was that this was the beginning of one of baseball's most incredible stories.

CHAPTER FOUR

Idaho Falls

IT WAS THE TAIL END OF THE SEASON WHEN BILLY MARTIN arrived at Idaho Falls, and he was immediately pressed into service, replacing the ballplayer who had been injured. In the very first inning of his first professional game, Billy showed the kind of innate skill and craftiness that stamped him as a future major-league star.

He was playing third base. The opposing team had a man on first, and one out. The batter got hold of an inside pitch and smashed a vicious drive down the third-base line. It was a foul ball, perhaps by inches, but Billy, who saw the ball barely go foul, made a great one-handed stop and whipped the ball to second to start a double play. Then, without so much as a side glance at the umpire, he trotted into the dugout. Strictly sandlot stuff, but it worked. The inning was over. The umpire was fooled and never called the ball foul. Billy had completely hoodwinked him.

Billy played 32 games for Idaho Falls as a young rookie and he was just adequate on the field and at bat. He hit for a .254 average and was charged with 16 errors; that's an average of an error every 2 games.

He wasn't too happy with his performance. He wasn't comfortable with the men he played with, either. There weren't any of his hometown pals to bounce around with, and all the Idaho Falls men were much older than he was, still a teen-ager. He could go into the bars with them, but he couldn't drink with them. And despite the fact that his life had been largely influenced by two women, his mother and grandmother, or maybe because of it, he couldn't join his teammates in the girl game.

He had a difficult time dealing with girls.

"The truth is," says Billy Martin, "I was afraid of girls. I didn't know how to handle them. Even talk to them. I was lonely and anxious to make good."

In truth, too, Billy's world had been largely a man's world: the gang on his street, basketball, football, baseball. He hadn't ever taken a girl to any of the school dances, and not only because he couldn't afford the price of the tickets or a hamburger and Coke after the dance. It may have seemed ridiculous to fans who watched his aggressiveness on the field, but Billy Martin was self-conscious, shy, and insecure in the company of women.

At any rate, he would not join his teammates when they went around womanizing, which was a constant activity of the Idaho Falls squad; he didn't even try, and he took a lot of ribbing from the older men because of it.

The ribbing, however, was to take a sudden turn, and abruptly, because of another of the rarely recognized traits of Billy Martin: a touch of generosity.

There was a certain restaurant the ballplayers frequented. Perhaps the attraction was a pretty little waitress at the restaurant, and everyone on that Idaho Falls club, except Billy, had tried to date her. But the waitress, as attractive as she was, was not to be had. All she gave the hungry ballplayers and their subtle and not so subtle invitations was that pretty waitress smile of hers.

It was different between the pretty waitress and Billy.

Birthdays are special events. Billy Martin is sentimental about birthdays. He learned one day it was the waitress's birthday and he was too tongue-tied to tell her that he wished her the best, and too timid to send her a bouquet of flowers or a box of candy. He left a dollar at his plate on the table, just as a token of how he felt about her birthday.

"Hey," shouted the waitress, cleaning up the dishes, and just as Billy was about to leave the restaurant. "You left a dollar here!"

"No," said Billy, scarcely louder than a whisper. "That's for your birthday."

The waitress didn't have time to say thank you. Billy was out of the door and gone before she could open her mouth.

The next day, however, before Billy could board the team bus, heading for a road trip, the little waitress grabbed him.

"Here's something for good luck," she said, and embraced him and gave him a big, warm kiss on the lips.

"Say hey!" yelled the boys on the bus. "You're doing all right, aren't you?"

"What's been going on between you and that pretty little thing in the restaurant?"

"Nothing," said Billy, blushing and embarrassed. "Absolutely nothing."

"Oh yeah? Tell that to your mamma!"

All the way down to the next town and the next game, they kidded Billy about his romance; and Billy stopped trying to convince them that there was nothing between him and the waitress. He began to enjoy his embarrassment. He was a man now, and he enjoyed that feeling of being a man among men. It had been some time in coming.

But that was one of the very few experiences Billy enjoyed, playing for the Idaho Falls club. His performance with the Pioneer League club didn't promise anything more than another season with Idaho Falls, and for all his love of the game, Billy didn't relish the prospect of another season with what was definitely bush league. Fortunately, there was another destination for Billy Martin in 1947.

Perhaps it was Billy's drive, his hustle and spirit—perhaps Billy reminded Casey of his own youth; whatever the reason, Casey wanted another look at "the fresh kid." He had him report to the Oakland Oaks for spring training.

For Martin, the call came like a message from heaven.

"I figured I was now in the biggest league I'd ever see," says Billy. "I kept telling myself that I was as good as any other guy playing for Oakland. Maybe not better, but just as good."

On the West Coast, before the Dodgers moved to Los Angeles in 1958 and the Giants to San Francisco, before the expansion put other big-league clubs on the coast, the Pacific

Coast League, with such fine clubs as the San Francisco Seals (where Joe DiMaggio got his start in baseball), the Hollywood Stars, Portland, San Diego, Seattle, Sacramento, Los Angeles, and Oakland provided outstanding baseball for most coast fans and was the only league for the fans, who seldom got to see *the* major-league teams in action.

Billy Martin was in his glory, and Casey Stengel went out of his way to make the Kid feel he belonged.

"He knew that I needed attention. For all my cockiness, he knew that I needed a pat on the back every once in a while to keep me going," says Billy Martin. "He encouraged me. He became like a father to me."

That Billy Martin subconsciously missed his own father when he was a boy is obvious enough. It becomes obvious, studying the man, that his aggressiveness on the field, his battles with club owners, umpires, and anyone else with authority concealed a profound and deeply rooted insecurity that never left him.

Casey, instinctively, recognized that insecurity. Maybe it was an echo of his own insecurity. In any case, he never let Billy think he was being neglected, though he did that bit of service for the youngster in his own queer way. Queer way, of course, was always the one and only way for the former left-handed dental student who became a legend on the diamond.

"Martin!" he yelled one fine afternoon, during a tight training-camp ball game. "Get over here!"

"I jumped up off the bench," says Martin; he had been getting splinters in his pants, watching the game. "I was sure Casey wanted me to pinch-hit."

He had the whole script written before he got to Casey. He was going to hit a homer and win the game. And Casey was going to pat him on the head and say, "That's my boy!"

But Casey had a completely different script ready for the boy.

"Stick around, kid," he said, his eyes glued on what was happening on the field. "I may need you to umpire."

Billy got used to the way the old man kidded him. He recognized the affection behind it, and Billy, always hungry for affection, ate it up. Besides, he often gave Casey as much as he got.

There was the time Casey was out on the field with him, showing him some of the more subtle points in making the double play.

"What's the matter with the way I do it?" demanded the Kid.

"You're not on the dance floor jitterbugging, kiddo," snapped Casey.

"Don't knock it if you can't do it," Martin snapped back.

"If it was any other kid," said Casey, telling the story long after, "I'd tell him to take off his uniform and clear out of the park. Not this kid. He wants to play ball so bad, it sticks out all over him. And I love him for his lip. Look at the way he studies every pitch," said Casey. "That's a smart ballplayer for you."

Billy knew that fast-ball pitchers tired in the late innings and that a smart hitter could pull the ball in those late innings. He shifted his position in the field accordingly.

Casey roomed him with Cookie Lavagetto. He couldn't have done any better for Billy. Cookie had been a fine ballplayer, and now in the twilight of his career Cookie was playing out the string at Oakland. And Cookie, too, marveled about young Billy Martin.

"I never knew a young ballplayer who was so eager to learn everything he might about the game. The only thing he talked about was baseball, and from the minute we got into the room until we left it; and then all the way to the ball field."

"I'll be grateful forever," said Billy Martin, "for Casey rooming me with Lavagetto; and to Cookie for all the help he gave me."

One time Cookie Lavagetto said to Billy, "There are a lot of fellows with all the ability it takes to play in the major leagues, but they never make it, they always get stuck in the minor leagues because they haven't got the guts to make the climb."

Billy Martin never forgot that bit of wisdom, not that he

ever lacked the guts, but it strengthened him in his determination, and made him realize the importance of his will, sheer will, to succeed in the goal he had set for himself.

As spring training for the Oakland Oaks came to its inevitable close, Billy Martin was sure he would be included on the club's roster for the 1947 season. The way he had been playing, the attention he had gotten from Cookie Lavagetto, and the individual attention and coaching Casey Stengel had given him made him certain he had won himself a spot on the team.

But Casey didn't see it quite the way Billy saw it. Casey felt that the young fellow needed another year of seasoning, more playing time, that he might lose some of his brash confidence, some of his brazen self-assurance, sitting on the bench and not playing regularly.

He sent him down to the Phoenix club in the Class C Arizona-Texas League. The Arizona-Texas League was a faster league than the Idaho Falls team that Billy played with the previous year.

Casey thought the move would do the kid good, give him more playing time in a faster league with more experienced players; but Billy Martin didn't like it. He felt that he was as good as any man on Casey Stengel's squad, and that he was getting a raw deal.

"You sure blew one," he shot at Casey, angrily, before he hopped the train for Arizona.

But Casey, as almost always, was right in his judgment, and Billy Martin was to recognize the wisdom of that judgment as he flashed through a brilliant season with Phoenix that summer of '47.

CHAPTER FIVE

The Oaks

BILLY MARTIN'S MANAGER AT PHOENIX WAS ARKY BIGGS, A HELL-to-leather ballplayer.

"Knock 'em down!" was his war cry, and that's the way his team played.

The Phoenix team was known as the Junior Gas House Gang.

Billy played third, Biggs played second, and Billy was in his element. The rough, tough game was his style, and Arky didn't have to encourage his third baseman very much to play "knock 'em down" baseball.

One night, when Phoenix was playing at Bisbee, Arky Biggs tangled with someone who played the game as hard as he asked of his own men, catcher Clint Courtney; Courtney came into second, his spikes riding high, and cut up Arky's legs bad. "Almost cut off Biggs's legs," Billy Martin says.

Arky Biggs, in any case, was cut up so badly that he had to sit out the rest of the season. Billy Martin was moved over to second base.

It wasn't his best position at the time.

"I made 55 errors," says Billy, "and it cost us the pennant."

Despite all the errors, it was a great year for the young ball-player. He hit for a .392 average and batted in 174 runs, leading the Arizona-Texas League in both categories. He hit safely 230 times, which was a record for the league, led the league with 48 doubles, and stole 31 bases. He had 317 assists and 207 putouts. He was voted the Most Valuable Player in the league for 1947.

At the award dinner, which Casey Stengel, Brick Laws,

Cookie Lavagetto, and other big brass out of Oakland at-
tended, Billy was called to the dais to receive the MVP plaque.

There were tears in Billy's eyes. It took him a while before
he could open his mouth, and when he did, all he could say,
pointing to the plaque, was, "It says here that I batted .392.
Somebody made a mistake. I batted .394."

Casey had an observation for that performance.

"I heard it. I heard it all. After that, nobody had to tell me
that that kid was not a big-leaguer."

Martin reported to the Oaks' spring-training camp in 1948
determined to stick with the team, and he was so impressive in
those early team drills that Casey kept him with the team.
Billy was ready for Triple-A ball. When Dario Lodigiani, the
Oaks' second baseman, got hurt early in the season, Billy was
inserted into the lineup at second base, and when Lodigiani returned, Billy remained a regular for the rest of the year, playing second, third, or short.

Because of his aggressive play and cocky attitude, Billy took
more than his share of ridicule from opposing players. They
called attention to his big nose and jug ears, and Billy took the
riding within limits.

He recalls one of his fights, early on in that first year with
Oakland, with special satisfaction.

"Who do you think was the first guy out there, swinging and
backing me up? Casey!"

The old man still had the old blood and guts in him, and always would have, even if his legs were slower getting him out
into the middle of a melee.

There was one incident that came at a most inopportune
moment for Billy Martin. It was an incident that almost put
him out of baseball for good.

Several big-league scouts had been following Martin's play
and were impressed. One scout had already made an offer to
purchase Billy's contract from Oakland for fifty thousand dollars.

But in a game against the Hollywood Stars, a Hollywood

player came tearing into second base, spiked Billy about both legs, and forced him from the game.

"There was blood all over me," says Billy.

They got him into the dressing room. They called for a doctor from the stands. They gave him a good shot of whiskey and four guys held him down as the doctor stitched him up without benefit of an anesthetic.

"I didn't holler," says Martin.

But the injury, which forced him out of the lineup, was enough to cool the ardor of the big-league scouts who had shown an interest in Billy.

Still, Billy hit for a .277 average that 1948 season with Oakland, and his spirited play sparked the Oaks to the Pacific Coast League pennant. It was the first pennant the club had won in twenty-one years.

The New York Yankee owners were impressed enough with that championship to bring old Casey back to the major leagues, as manager of the New York Yankees. And where Casey went, in those years, Billy Martin was sure to follow.

But not just yet.

Billy had another year with the Oakland Oaks, this time under manager Charlie Dressen.

Chuck Dressen was fast-talking, glib, aggressive, and possessed an ego as big as anyone who ever played or managed in baseball. He was a gambler, to boot.

He couldn't hit major-league pitching with any sort of consistency, and after eight years he was through as a player. But that wasn't the end of baseball for Dressen. He borrowed the money to pay his own way to Nashville, in the Southern Association, when he heard they were looking for a manager, and sold himself to Fay Murray, who owned the Vols.

"How do you know you can manage a club?" asked Murray.

"I tell you what," came back the gambling Dressen. "Make me the manager of your club and if it doesn't win more than half its games, which is a lot better than they're doing right now, you won't need to pay me a dime in salary; just pay my expenses here; that's all."

Chuck Dressen got the job and went on to become one of the more successful managers in baseball. If any two men were meant to work together, Billy Martin and Chuck Dressen were all of that, and more.

At first, Dressen wasn't all sold on the brassy, belligerent Martin. Dressen knew that Billy was Casey Stengel's pet ballplayer and he took Casey's evaluation of Martin as a ballplayer with a grain of salt. But Dressen quickly learned that Billy was exactly the kind of ballplayer he needed to put together a winning team.

Just a couple of days before the opening of the season, the Oaks' A squad played an exhibition game against the Cleveland Indians, at Oakland. It was a morning game. The B squad, with Cookie Lavagetto managing, was scheduled for an afternoon game that same day in Stockton.

"I'd like to drive out to Stockton," Billy said, "if it's all right with you."

"You got a girl in Stockton?" said Dressen.

"Nah," said Billy the Kid. "I was just thinking that Cookie might be able to use me in their game. I got nothing else to do."

That was enough to impress Chuck Dressen.

"Anybody who wants to play ball that bad," he said to anybody willing to listen, "belongs on my team."

They became a pair, and if Billy needed any further lessons in aggressive baseball, in Dressen he had a manager who knew every trick, every strategy in the book.

"Take charge!" he would yell at Martin. "Don't you give the other fellow an inch! Talk back to them! Holler! Fight 'em! Don't give an inch!"

Under Casey Stengel's crafty leadership, Martin became the team scrapper. He would taunt and yell and hustle from the moment he stepped across the diamond. Now under Dressen's urging, Billy quickly became the most aggressive "holler" man on the team, and it was logical, for Dressen and Stengel were aggressive, fiery scrappers as players, and when both men became big-league managers, they demanded aggressive, fiery play from their players. And in Martin they had their finest pupil.

Sometimes, of course, aggression and aggression clashed, and so did Billy and his manager.

Walt Dropo, playing for Sacramento at the time, threw a body block at Billy one afternoon. Billy took a big lead off first, after singling through the middle. The Sacramento pitcher snapped the ball to Dropo, playing first base, and Dropo threw his huge six-foot, five-inch body at Martin, to knock him off the base. He was at least seventy-five pounds heavier than the Kid, but Billy managed to get back to the bag and, later in the game, he tried to pay back Dropo.

It was in the ninth inning. Oakland was leading by one run. With one out, Dropo reached first on a single. The next batter rapped a sharp grounder to short; the shortstop whipped the ball to Martin at second for a force. Billy had a double play in his hands but, instead of throwing it to first, he whipped the ball right at the head of the oncoming Walt Dropo. He missed Dropo, fortunately for Walt, and for Billy as well; but he also missed first base.

Instead of the double play and the game, Sacramento still had a man on first.

Dressen blew a fuse in the dugout.

Happily, the next man for Sacramento was an easy out and Oakland took the game, but Charlie Dressen was hot under the collar.

Billy Martin was undressing when Dressen confronted him.

"What the hell made you do that? You don't mess up a double play to bean somebody. What the hell do you think you were doing?"

"Aw, shut up!" came back Billy Martin. He was still fuming about the block Walt Dropo had thrown at him. "What do you know about baseball?" he yelled at his manager, and headed into the showers.

Dressen followed him, right into the showers, still completely dressed in his baseball uniform.

"I'll tell you what I know about baseball!" yelled Charlie

Dressen, the water pouring down on him. "Pull another stunt like that and you go back to Idaho Falls!"

Charlie couldn't quite hear what Billy Martin came back with, but he heard enough of the foul reply to slap a fine on the fresh kid.

"If you don't apologize fast, it'll cost you two hundred dollars!"

Billy's answer was to tell his manager where to hang his hat and shove his glove, and a few other words of similar advice. Perhaps it was fortunate that Chuck Dressen didn't hear any of it.

Still fuming, and sure that it was no apology that Billy Martin was offering, Dressen stepped out of the shower and for the first time realized he was wringing wet.

The morning after, Billy, still as mad as a hornet, walked into Brick Laws's office. He counted out twenty ten-dollar bills and dropped them on his desk.

"What's this for?" asked Laws.

"I'm paying off the fine Chuck Dressen laid on me," said Billy.

"Take it back," said Brick Laws, shoving the money to Billy. "We take your fines off your paycheck."

Sometime later, probably prompted by the cool head of Cookie Lavagetto, Billy caught up with his manager.

"I'd like to say something," he said.

"Go ahead and say it," said Chuck Dressen.

It wasn't easy for Billy Martin, especially with a gang of his teammates around, but he said it anyway.

"I'm sorry," he blurted, "for what I said to you yesterday."

Dressen grinned. He liked the Kid.

"Thanks," he said. "And you've just saved yourself two hundred dollars."

"I admired the Kid's guts," said Charlie Dressen.

And Billy Martin said, "Dressen helped me, just like Casey. He taught me how to hit to right field, how to hit behind a runner, and how to avoid the runner coming in to second base, and get the ball to first base for the double play. Maybe I was

Twenty-one-year-old Billy Martin, scrappy second baseman of the champion Oakland, California, Oaks, and Jackie Jensen, hard-hitting Oaks outfielder, ready to report to the New York Yankees in 1950. The two Oakland stars were sold to the Yankees for a reported sum of $75,000. Martin, from Berkeley, signed by the Oaks in 1946, wasn't too happy about leaving Oakland. "I love this team and this town. This is my home. I don't know about New York." Jensen was an all-American halfback at the University of California before turning to professional baseball.

March 3, 1950, Phil Rizzuto, crack shortstop, and Billy Martin, rookie second baseman, pose "working out" at the Yankees' spring training camp at St. Petersburg, Florida.

March 19, 1954, Fort Ord, California. Billy Martin, former Yankees star second baseman, looks wistfully at a pair of his old baseball shoes while getting used to his new uniform—an Army one issued by Uncle Sam at Fort Ord, where he is engaged in basic training.

October 2, 1955, Colorado Springs. With papers in hand, Billy Martin prepares to leave Fort Carson, Colorado, for the last time. Martin after eighteen months in the Army will join his New York Yankees teammates in San Francisco.

September 2, 1955. Yankees manager Casey Stengel beckons to Billy Martin after a pre-game practice at Yankee Stadium. Billy returned to the Yankee lineup after more than a year in the Army. He played shortstop and batted third as the Yankees opened a series with the Washington Senators.

September 3, 1976. Twenty-one years later Billy is shown alongside a picture of Casey Stengel in his office at Yankee Stadium. Billy as manager of the Yankees led his team to the championship of the Eastern Division as the season ended.

July 25, 1957. New York Yankees star Mickey Mantle shows fellow ballplayers the organizational brochure of the Mickey Mantle Fund for Research in Hodgkins Disease at a luncheon in New York City. Mantle, whose father died of the disease, is chairman of the foundation. Left to right are Mantle, ex-Yankee Billy Martin, with Kansas City, Hank Bauer, Bill Skowron, Yogi Berra, and Jerry Coleman. *(A.P. Photo)*

Cleveland's star second baseman, Billy Martin, and airline stewardess Gretchen Winkler pictured above at New York's Harwyn Club announced their marriage to local newsmen. The couple were married in Las Vegas, October 10, 1959. Mickey Mantle was Martin's best man and Miss Winkler's sister, Karen Carr, was maid of honor. *(Harwyn Club Photo)*

an aggressive player when I came up to Oakland; Dressen smartened me up, taught me some finesse, and made me a smoother, smarter ballplayer."

Billy improved in all departments under Dressen. He hit for an average of .286, slammed 12 home runs, batted in 92 runs, and led the league in putouts by a second baseman.

At a night game in Oakland, late in the season, a blimp floated over the ball park. It was a blimp that spelled out late news flashes and advertisements of all sorts in electric lights. This night, as it hovered over the game, the lights read: "Billy Martin Sold to Yankees."

The crowd roared and Billy Martin looked up to see why.

He was perhaps the most puzzled person in the park, reading that message. It was the first word he had heard about the deal. Sure, he was excited. Every ballplayer dreams of playing in the big leagues; but Oakland was home for Billy Martin. He was comfortable in Oakland. He loved Oakland. He loved playing in Oakland before his friends and family.

There were other things about the Yankee deal, he would learn later, factors that disturbed him and caused him to question the deal.

He learned that he was just an added throw-in that included the sale of Oakland's hard-hitting outfielder, Jackie Jensen. Billy Martin didn't consider himself "throw-in" material.

Second, Jensen was getting a $65,000 bonus. Billy wasn't getting a bonus of any kind, and this didn't sit well with the Kid. He had played better ball than Jackie, even outhit him with his .286 average to Jensen's .261.

Third, Billy would have to take a cut in salary. He was getting $9,000 at Oakland; he would get only $7,500 with the Yankees.

And finally, he didn't see why he had to leave his family and home grounds, move three thousand miles across the country, to prove again that he was a good ballplayer.

But Casey Stengel wanted the Kid with him in New York. And if Casey Stengel called, Billy Martin, whatever his doubts and resentment, would answer.

"If Casey asked me to run through a brick wall," said Billy Martin at one time or another, "I'd be out there, trying to run through that wall."

Casey had led the Yankees to a pennant in 1949, and wanted Billy to play for him. That ultimately was enough of a reason to leave Oakland, his home. Now Billy Martin was on his way to New York to play for the world champion Yankees.

CHAPTER SIX

A Fresh Young Kid
with the Yankees

EVERYBODY IN THE YANKEES' ORGANIZATION—PLAYERS AND FRONT office—knew all about Billy Martin long before they assembled for spring training in 1950. Casey Stengel had been singing the praises of the young Oakland ballplayer from the moment he arrived in 1949 to take charge of the Bronx Bombers.

"He's a battler," said Case. "He's got heart. He's fresh, and he's smart. He knows what he's doing at second and he plays the game good."

Before the Kid set foot in the Yankees' camp for spring training, everyone knew that Martin was Casey's pet.

"Mr. Billy Stengel," they called him.

"The freshest kid which ever played for me," was the way Casey introduced him to Arthur Daley of the New York *Times*, and to every other member of the sports press in camp.

Mickey Mantle, who was in the Yankees' camp as a rookie in 1950, tells just how fresh the Kid was.

"I'd always heard how smart Frank Crosetti was and that he was the man who was mainly responsible for the great double-play combination the Yankees had at short and second base.

"Well, Billy Martin and I are listening to Crosetti teaching the best way to make the double play, and Billy stops Crosetti and tells Frankie he's got it all wrong.

"I didn't know Billy then, and I just stood there, struck dumb, thinking how this smart-aleck son-of-a-bitch can have the gall to tell the great Frank Crosetti how to make the double play."

Fresh. Brash. Cocky. He was all that . . . and more.

From the minute Billy put on a Yankee uniform, he felt and acted like a regular. And he let everyone in camp know just how he felt. If any of the veterans came near second base, he growled, angrily, and let them know he didn't like it. Second base was his, as far as he was concerned, and he wanted everyone to know that, too.

When he was assigned to an upper berth during the spring-training trips, he opened his mouth and hollered.

Rookies are not supposed to complain about anything, but Billy didn't know it or, more likely, he wasn't going to keep his mouth shut about anything he didn't like.

He complained to Bill McCorry, the road secretary.

"Lower berths are for regulars," said McCorry, politely.

That was no explanation for Billy Martin.

"And what the hell makes you think I'm not a regular?" he snapped at the secretary.

Of course he didn't get the lower berth, but that didn't stop Billy from jawing.

He couldn't be kept off the field, even when he wasn't needed, even when he wasn't wanted.

One afternoon he picked up the ball and trotted out to the pitcher's mound to throw batting practice. Anything to get some action, give him a feeling of active participation.

"Get off the mound!" yelled the Yankees' pitching coach, Jim Turner.

Billy took one look at the fellow who was trying to order him around. He recognized the pitching coach, but that made no difference to his angry response.

"Who the hell are you, telling me what to do?" he snapped. "When you're managing this club, then you can tell me!"

The veteran Yankees didn't take kindly to the "fresh kid." There were exceptions, of course; particularly Joe DiMaggio, who took him under his wing and practically adopted the brash youngster.

Huge Johnny Mize, generally a gentle person until aroused, took immediate exception to the arrogant, fresh rookie.

Mize was generally late for the road-trip bus, and nobody minded much, except Billy Martin. Once, as Johnny walked up the bus steps just about ten minutes late, the fresh kid yelled at him, "Now Big John! Give us a few thousand words!"

The slugger's face turned red.

"Why you little bush bastard," he spat, and took his seat.

For once Billy kept his mouth shut, or, more likely, some older and wiser counsel told him to shut up.

In fact, despite the cockiness of the kid, his insolence and the sass he tossed around with reckless abandon, the veterans began by degrees to tolerate, then enjoy the rookie and his antics. In some ways he was a novelty in the Yankee camp. There hadn't been anyone like him around the Yankees since the days Leo (the Lip) Durocher wore a Yankee uniform in 1925.

They rode Billy enough about the size of his nose, his jug ears, his size, and his weight, but they also recognized him as an asset for the club, a needle, a spur to their game.

With Phil Rizzuto, Jerry Coleman, and George Stirnweiss, all outstanding Yankees, it was tough for Billy Martin to break into the regular lineup. He did go North with the club but, for all the obvious attention Casey showered on his rookie, Billy was only used as a pinch-hitter, pinch-runner, an occasional substitute for an injured player during the entire 1950 baseball season.

Casey Stengel's Yankees had won the 1949 pennant on the last day of the season. They had come down to the last two games of the season one full game behind the Boston Red Sox. All Boston had to do was win one of those games to hold the lead and take the flag; they couldn't do it. Or rather, Casey's Yankees wouldn't let them do it.

In the first of those last two games, the Yanks overcame a 4–0 deficit to win, 5–4, leaving Boston and New York in a flat tie for the league lead.

In the second game, it was all Vic Raschi, with the Yankees scoring four runs in the eighth to take a 5–0 lead; but it wasn't all over, not yet.

In the ninth, Raschi, who had given up only two hits,

relaxed, and the Red Sox jumped on him. They scored three runs, had a man on first, and the possible tying run, Birdie Tebbetts, at the plate with two men out.

Yogi Berra walked slowly to the mound to slow down Raschi, say a few encouraging words.

"Gimme the goddamn ball and get the hell out of here!" yelled the quick-tempered pitcher, spitting the tobacco juice out of his mouth.

Tommy Henrich had started from his first-base position toward the mound, but changed his mind quickly.

Raschi pitched. Tebbetts took his full cut. The ball sailed high and foul just behind second base. Henrich moved back for it, but Jerry Coleman, yelling all the way, called him off, and squeezed the ball for the final out, victory, and the pennant.

Coach Bill Dickey jumped up in the air for joy, hit his head against the dugout roof, and knocked himself unconscious.

Casey said, "And to think they're paying me for managing so great a bunch of boys."

In the first game of the 1950 season, the Red Sox, still chafing from that 1949 last-game-of-the-season defeat, welcomed the Yankees to Fenway Park in Boston with something less than love in their hearts.

They went after the Yankees' ace pitcher, Allie Reynolds, right from the start, and the New York bullpen couldn't stop them until they had a lead of 9-0.

That's when Billy Martin entered the picture, cocky and brash as ever.

On the way up from training camp, someone asked him whether he wasn't excited about going to New York.

"What for?" he asked, looking up from the magazine he was reading. "I've seen it all in the pictures."

When he was asked whether Yankee Stadium didn't give him a bit of the jitters, he said, "It's a ball park, isn't it? Why should I get the jitters? As long as it's a ball park, I can play in it, and hit in it."

Nothing seemed to faze the Kid, not even the Red Sox'

twenty-five-game winner, Mel Parnell. And Billy didn't figure that Casey had sent him in to pinch-hit in the eighth because the game was lost anyway. If Billy Martin ever sensed that others might not respect his ability as a ballplayer, he never for a moment lost confidence in himself as a player.

It was his first appearance at the plate at Boston's Fenway Park, but he stepped in to hit with the poise of a veteran, and on the first pitch he smashed a line drive that bounced against the left-field wall, sending two runners across the plate.

"Atta boy, kiddo!" yelled Casey, pleased with his protégé, even if the Yankees were still losing a game he wanted especially to win.

But that wasn't the end of Billy's first day as a Yankee.

The Yankees batted around in that eighth inning in Boston and Martin came up for a second at-bat, this time with the bases loaded.

It wasn't Parnell pitching anymore; the Boston bullpen was working. That made no difference to Billy Martin.

"Pitchers are all the same. They throw the ball," he explained. "You've just got to know how to hit them."

And once again he smashed out a hit, two out of two in his first major-league game, sending in yet another Yankee run.

"Pretty good way to break in, kid," said Joe DiMaggio, as the rookie trotted back into the dugout at the end of the inning.

Casey was jubilant. Not only was his boy doing all right, but the Yankees won that opener in Fenway Park, 15–10.

The Yankees were loaded with talented players, however, and Billy did not play again for almost a month. Then, in a game against Cleveland, Billy hit a three-run homer to win the game.

Casey sent him in to pinch-hit once more, this time against the St. Louis Browns in the tenth inning, and once again he singled home the winning run.

This was May 13. Despite the fact that he wasn't in the regular lineup, Billy had reason to feel good about himself. He was performing the way he was supposed to perform, when he was called off the bench to deliver. But the next day, May 14, the roof fell on him.

May 14, Billy Martin never forgot that day, Casey Stengel called him into his office.

"Billy," said Casey, in his most fatherlike manner, "we're going to send you down to Kansas City."

Billy was too stunned by the announcement to open his mouth on it.

"That's Triple-A, you know," said Casey.

Billy was furious, but he still kept his mouth shut. Being sent down was the last thing he expected. It was the feeling that he was getting the dirty end of the stick that got him. He was more inclined to let the tears run down his face than to holler at Casey.

Casey, uncomfortable and very unhappy, did as well as he could, tried to explain things to the kid he loved like a son.

"We've got to cut somebody and we want to sell George Stirnweiss, but we've used up all our options on him. We've still got options on you. We sell Stirnweiss for twenty-five thousand dollars and we'll have you back in thirty days. How does it sound to you?"

Billy didn't have to think and he knew that it didn't matter how it sounded to him.

He felt licked, and he had never felt licked before.

"If it's got to be," he said finally, "it's got to be," and he turned to leave the office as quickly as his feet would carry him. For all the anger in him, he loved Casey too much to make it any harder for the manager.

And old Case stopped him before he could get to the door.

"I don't like it, Billy any more'n you do," he said. "You go up to the front office and tell Mr. George Weiss and Mr. Dan Topping you don't think this is fair."

And that's what Billy Martin did, and it haunted him for the rest of his career.

"I took a cut in salary to come here," he argued with George Weiss. "It's not fair you sending me down."

For George Weiss, general manager of the New York club, the Yankees were an aristocratic, reserved coterie of gentlemen. He didn't care for Stengel's roughhouse style of play. A Yankee player was a gentleman, on and off the field, and Weiss cared less for fresh, brash, aggressive young rookies. He disliked Martin at first sight.

And Billy Martin didn't like George Weiss's coolness, indifference, his sharpness at contract time. Billy's tongue grew sharper as his face got redder. He was so mad that the tears rushed up into his eyes.

"I'll make you sorry for this!" he yelled at the calm and collected George Weiss, and he slammed the door behind him.

Later, talking about the episode, Billy Martin said, "It didn't occur to me that Casey might have had ulterior motives, that Casey was using him to battle the front office without having to do the dirty work himself. It really worked both ways. Whenever Casey and Weiss had a battle, they used me to get at each other."

But Casey did keep his word to Billy Martin. Billy hit .280 in 29 games for Kansas City and, within a month, he was back with the Yankees.

Still, there were Coleman and Stirnweiss, and Billy saw little action in the field that year. He did develop, however, with the encouragement of his crusty old manager, into a first-rate bench jockey.

"I've got a job for you," Casey would say. "Get on Al Rosen. Ride him. He's the big star of the Clevelands and he's mean with that bat."

And Billy made a good job of it, making Al Rosen, the star third baseman of the Cleveland Indians, miserable for nine innings.

In an exhibition game with the Dodgers, Billy gave it to his rival second baseman, Jackie Robinson.

"If I was in your league, I'd have your job, fatso!"

If he couldn't play in the field, he had his own game to play.

"That fresh punk," said Casey, "how I love him."

Jackie Robinson, incidentally, was to speak up for Billy Martin on more than one occasion in later years.

"Billy," he said, "is not brash or a dead-end kid or any of the other things he has been called. He is a smart player, cool, calculating, always thinking, always daring, always looking for a way to win. A player like that gets to be a pain in the neck to some people, but it has nothing to do with the man. He has always played up to the fullest the times I played with him."

This was from one of the greatest players in the history of baseball, and one of the most courageous men to put on a baseball uniform.

And the kudos were undoubtedly well deserved, in later years. In 1950, Billy Martin just warmed the bench for the most part, as Casey Stengel led the Yankees to their second straight pennant. Billy sat on the bench as the Yankees beat the Philadelphia Phillies in four straight games to win the World Series.

Billy's fame, and notoriety, were still a couple of baseball seasons away.

Meanwhile, there was to be one happy moment, if only a temporarily happy moment in his life, as well as an aborted stint with the United States Army.

CHAPTER SEVEN

"The Three Musketeers"

BACK HOME IN WEST BERKELEY, AFTER THE 1950 SEASON, BILLY Martin married the girl he left behind him, Lois Berndt. Billy was twenty-two, Lois was eighteen. Billy, for all his rough and readiness to fight on the field, for all his seemingly immature, boyish aggressiveness, understood the meaning of the marriage vows and, from the very beginning, he was completely dedicated to them. Lois, still no more than a teen-ager, may have understood the vows as well as Billy, and been dedicated to them, but she wasn't ready for, and never was able to take the kind of life Billy had to lead as a ballplayer.

The Korean conflict had warmed up in the summer of 1950, and Billy, along with such Yankee stars as Whitey Ford, Bobby Brown, and Jerry Coleman, were drafted into the Army.

Billy Martin didn't forget baseball, but he took to the Army in style—that is, in Billy Martin style. He became a good soldier and was popular with everyone in his company. He was a good storyteller and kept his fellow soldiers laughing night and day with stories of the great Joe DiMaggio, Tommy Henrich, Yogi Berra, and the other Yankee stars.

Then, one day in Camp Ord, California, where Billy had been stationed, he got a letter from home he didn't know quite how to handle.

It was a letter from his mother, detailing the difficulties the family was having at home in West Berkeley. His stepfather had a serious asthmatic attack and was too sick to look for a job. There were his younger brother and sister who had to be fed and clothed. They were having a very rough time of it.

"We'd never been on relief," said Billy Martin. "We'd always been poor, but somehow there was always enough to eat at home, and I didn't wear the best clothes but I wasn't ashamed of what I was wearing when I went to school."

The letter troubled him, deeply. He took the letter to his captain.

"Could you send all my pay back home?" he asked.

"Sure," said the captain. "It wouldn't help much. You couldn't support a family like that on a private's pay. Let me look into it."

It didn't take the captain long to carry out a formal investigation, and in a few days Billy received a hardship discharge from the Army.

Billy Martin had served twenty-seven weeks in Uncle Sam's service. He was back with the Yankees in the spring of 1951.

The prospects for Billy breaking into the regular lineup in '51 weren't much better than they were in '50. Bobby Brown, Jerry Coleman, Gil McDougald, and the veteran Phil Rizzuto were all with the club, and pretty well fixed in the New York infield.

Bobby Brown, who was still to be called up by the Army, traveled to Tulane to get his doctorate in medicine; Billy took his spot. But when Bobby returned to New York, Billy was back on the bench.

"You know," said Casey, "he wouldn't talk to me. He's my boy but for three days he wouldn't talk to me because I took him out of the lineup. I didn't talk to him either. But, just between you and me, I loved it."

And when he did sub for Bobby Brown, Casey had him hitting eighth. Billy Martin stormed up to his old manager, yelling, "Why the hell are you having me bat eighth?"

"I'm still managing this ball club, kiddo," said Casey.

"Why don't you have me bat after the batboy?" slapped the fresh kid.

"And where would you like me have you bat?" queried old Case. "Fourth? Clean-up?"

"Yeah!" said the brash young Martin, and that's where he thought he belonged, fourth.

It wasn't easy for Billy sitting out all those games, but he can recall with considerable pleasure that he shared the bench much of the time with Mickey Mantle, and that was the beginning of a great friendship.

To most of the Yankee players and would-be players converging on their Phoenix, Arizona, spring-training base, the name Mickey Mantle had little or no meaning. Most of them had never heard the name in the spring of 1951.

General manager George Weiss had the scouting report from scout Tom Greenwade that in essence stated, "I've come up with an eighteen-year-old kid who will be, in a couple of years, the greatest player in the game. When I first saw him," the report went on, "I knew how our scout Paul Kritchell felt when he first saw Lou Gehrig. He knew that as a baseball scout he would never have another moment in life like it. You know," said Greenwade, "I felt the same when I first saw Mantle play ball."

Mickey Mantle was born and brought up in Commerce, a rather drab town in the extreme northeastern part of Oklahoma with a mining population of some thirty-five hundred people. Mickey's father, Mutt Mantle, idolized Mickey Cochrane, the great Philadelphia Athletics' catcher, and named his newborn son Mickey after his idol.

Mickey was tutored by his father from the day he was old enough to hold a baseball bat properly, at the age of five. Mutt didn't want Mickey to waste out his life as a miner as he had, and so he patiently tutored the young boy in hitting . . . and from both sides of the plate, so that as a left-hand batter Mickey would have an advantage of the two or three steps closer to first base.

Mutt Mantle pitched to young Mickey every day for an hour or two. Most of the time the ball was a tennis ball, because it was easier on the neighbors' windows. In time, as the years rolled on, Mickey Mantle became an outstanding sandlot baseball player and the town's leading athlete.

At Commerce High, Mickey scored ten touchdowns in the six football games the school played. He pitched for the base-

ball team, and the team lost only to Miami High School, a
considerably larger school.

In 1949, after starring with the Baxter Spring Whizz Kids
baseball team, Mickey signed a Yankee contract that called for
a $1,100 bonus plus a salary of $140 per month.

Yankee scout Tom Greenwade didn't appreciate the full
significance of his coup that rainy afternoon in 1948 in that
parked car on the dusty street of Commerce, where he signed
Mantle. But it wasn't long before he realized that the shy,
smiling kid with shoulders like a Charles Atlas ad would one
day be placed in baseball's Hall of Fame alongside Babe Ruth,
Lou Gehrig, and Joe DiMaggio, and would become one of the
most popular ballplayers of his day.

That first year, in 1949, the Yankees sent Mickey to a Yankee farm team at Independence, Missouri, and there, under the
guidance and direction of Harry Craft, a former Kansas City
manager, Mickey played shortstop and finished the season with
a .313 batting average, while committing 47 errors. At season's
end Craft sent an enthusiastic report on Mantle to the Yankee
front office.

"Can be a great hitter," the report read. "Exceptional speed.
Just an average shortstop. Has a fine arm and a good pair of
hands. Attitude excellent. Will go all the way. Has everything
to be a great ballplayer. I would like to see him shifted to third
or outfield."

The following year the Yankees sent Mickey to Joplin, of
the Class C Western Association, where he blasted the league
apart with his incredible distance hitting, which included 26
homers and a .383 batting average as he led the team to the
championship of the league.

In the spring of 1951, Mickey was invited to report to the
Yankees' instructional camp at Phoenix, Arizona, but when
such rookies as Andy Carey, Tom Sturdivant, Bob Cerv, and
Tom Morgan appeared, Mickey was nowhere to be seen. Sev-
eral days passed, and when Mickey did not report, George
Weiss phoned him in Commerce.

"Mickey Mantle, what happened to you? When are you
coming to camp?" said the Yankees' general manager.

"I don't have any money for the fare to Phoenix," said Mickey. "I was supposed to get some bus tickets."

Weiss promptly wired the money to Mantle and within two days a shy, awkward Mickey Mantle ambled into the Yankees' camp at Phoenix.

The instructional camp devised by Stengel began immediately with foot races, and Mickey outran every player with ease. And when the batting drills began, Mickey's tremendous, long-distance hitting overshadowed everything in camp. That included Joe DiMaggio.

Casey had Tommy Henrich working with Mantle, and Tommy was patient and considerate of the shy slugger. Within a few days Mickey was moved to the outfield, where he would remain for the duration of his career with the Yankees.

Once he made the team, Mickey teamed up with another rookie, the glib, wisecracking Billy Martin, and the two youngsters quickly became the best of friends. Within a few days the two rookies became roommates, and though fundamentally Mickey didn't change, Billy Martin influenced the gawky, powerful Mantle and did bring about some changes in his lifestyle. During the six-year period that Billy played for the New York Yankees, he, Mickey, and Whitey Ford were to become fast friends. The three young players—Ford, the New York streetwise kid; Martin, the Berkeley dead-end kid; and Mantle, out of the mines in Commerce, became holy terrors in the locker rooms, hotels, and in the clubhouse. They drove Stengel frantic with their escapades, tricks on each other, playful fights, and just plain mischief, and they were dubbed "The Three Musketeers."

Billy Martin played in only fifty-one games for the Yankees in 1951, but in retrospect, Billy couldn't say that all the time he spent on the bench was wasted. Old Casey, with his uncanny understanding, felt that Martin, with his keen aptitude for the game, would someday make a fine coach or manager, and he fed the young player much of his knowledge. He had Billy sit next to him on the bench every day, listening and watching and listening and asking questions.

"He taught me so many things to watch on the field," said

Billy. "How to watch every move a pitcher makes. How to steal a base on a pitcher. How to watch the third-base coach and steal signals. How to help a pitcher out of a tight situation, to calm him down. When to take out a pitcher. How to use a relief pitcher."

When Case shifted the infield around for a certain batter, or placed an outfielder deep or shallow, he would explain the move to Martin. He would tell him why he was calling for a relief pitcher, why he'd signal a hit-and-run, a take, a steal. He used Billy as his messenger, too—to relay a message to a batter.

"Tell that fella up there to wait for a good pitch and hit a home run!" said Casey.

Andy Carey was at bat. There were two men on base, and Boston was ahead by two runs.

Andy had swung hard at a fast one and missed the ball by a mile.

Casey called time.

"Go ahead and tell him," yelled Casey, "to wait for a good pitch and hit a home run!"

Billy, still disbelieving what he heard, walked up to the plate and delivered the message, loud enough for Sammy White, the Red Sox catcher, to hear.

"You guys have got to be kidding," said Sammy White.

And Carey took the next pitch, then belted the following one for the home run Casey had ordered.

Sammy White just stood there, watching the ball go over the fence and not believing it.

Casey sat there on the bench and, soberly, explained to the amazed Billy Martin, "Just like slowing up an overanxious pitcher. You slowed him up pretty good."

When Martin came up to the plate, Sammy White, still not over it, said to him, "The funniest thing I've ever seen since I put on this mitt."

Said Billy, "When the old man tells us to do something, we just do it."

And so Billy sat on the bench next to Casey, listening, asking questions, observing every move the manager made. Billy also continued to take a lot of ribbing from the old manager.

For apparently no reason at all, Casey would suddenly turn on the Kid and say, "Now you take Ernie Lombardi who's a big man and has a big nose and you take Martin who's a little man and has a bigger nose. How do you figger it?"

And the fresh kid would come right back.

"And you take Stengel who's so in love with the game he carries a baseball in his sock."

Billy Martin was referring to the large lump on the old man's leg, but all's fair in love and war, and Casey loved that "fresh kid."

In 1952, Billy Martin would emerge from the relative obscurity of a part-time player to finally come into his own. It would be the year in which he would become the driving spark of the Yankee team. It was the year, too, in which he came of age and matured as a full-blown World Series hero.

CHAPTER EIGHT

"I Don't Care What They Call Me. . . ."

BILLY MARTIN STARTED THE 1952 SEASON DETERMINED TO WIN A starting position with the world champion New York Yankees. Jerry Coleman, the Yankees' regular second baseman, was to be inducted into the Marine Corps, and Billy was at his best in spring training. He drove at every ball hit to him as if his life depended on it. He worked the double play to perfection and, at bat, he sprayed line drives to all corners of the field. He was in good physical condition and he looked so fluid afield that at last Casey told him he would be the regular second baseman. And then all hell broke loose. He broke his ankle.

Joe DiMaggio had a television program, and of course Billy was glad to be one of his guests. Joe was demonstrating the different ways to slide into a base—that is, Joe was lecturing and Billy was demonstrating.

"Let's see Billy slide again," said the TV director taping the show. "We'd like another take on that action."

Billy obliged. There was nothing fake about Billy, on or off the field, and when he slid into the bag, he slid hard. He slid too hard on this one, caught his foot in the bag, and wound up with a broken ankle.

He didn't yell with pain; he yelled with frustration.

"With Coleman going into the Marines," said Casey, shaking his head, "and Brown going into the Army, I was figuring on McDougald at third base and Martin at second. And this thing had to happen."

The resultant inactivity gnawed at Martin, already a nervous, restless, eager performer. He feared that the Yankees would release him or perhaps buy another second baseman. In

62 days on the bench Martin's weight plummeted from 165 pounds to 131 pounds.

It didn't take long for Billy to break into the lineup Casey had figured for him once his ankle healed; and he was precisely what the manager wanted and needed. When Casey needed a batter to hit behind the runner and get him into scoring position, Billy was the man. He knew how to barrel into second when Casey needed someone to break up a double play. He was also the "policeman" for the club. When an opponent smashed into little Phil Rizzuto a bit harder than was deemed necessary, Billy was the man to pay off the "bully." Billy was also the "captain" of the Yankee bench jockeys. He could give a lot better than he received.

"You sons-of-bitches better watch out," warned Casey when the opposition jockeying got to be a little too raucous. "That Martin will get you!"

Billy was fearless. The size and weight of a player didn't scare him any.

"Hey Newk!" he needled Don Newcombe, the great, 225-pound Dodger hurler, as he warmed up for a World Series game against the Yanks. "There ain't no way you're getting out of this park until we rip you up. We've got all the gates locked."

"Come over here, little kid," said Newk. "I'll take you over my knee and spank you."

"And after that," came back brassy Billy Martin, "I'm going to beat the living shit out of you."

The Yankees were up in Boston's Fenway Park in June and the rookie Red Sox outfielder, Jimmy Piersall, was after Martin, riding him about the size of his nose . . . his ears.

The art of jockeying demands that your insults get your opponent mad, to unnerve and upset him so he can't think coolly and calmly. Jimmy Piersall didn't have the art down to a science; neither, for that matter, did Billy Martin.

The insults got hotter and more personal, till Billy invited Piersall to battle him under the stands.

This was all before the game got started, and Billy's invitation was actually intended as the ultimate insult. But Jimmy Piersall, who was in a particularly savage mood at the time, took up the invitation, and both men met under the stands.

Bill Dickey and Ellis Kinder started after them. This kind of fight wasn't exactly what either team wanted or needed. But before they could get to the two men, Billy had already knocked Piersall off his feet. Piersall didn't lack courage. He was up fast, and this time Billy hit him with a right and a left that bounced Piersall to his knees, the blood gushing from his mouth.

That was it. Dickey wrapped his big arms around the still-furious Billy Martin, and held him. Kinder took care of Piersall.

"I don't like to fight," said Billy, "and I don't care what they call me, so long as they don't get personal."

Maybe Billy Martin was serious, or maybe it was his sense of humor.

Casey, a rough-and-ready brawler in his prime as a ballplayer, was pleased with Billy's performance, and he didn't conceal his pleasure.

"This should wake my other tigers up," he said. "It's about time they realize they got to fight harder this year. I just hope that Martin's fighting spirit spreads to some of the others."

Then, with a twinkle in his eyes, he added, "I'll have to ask him to confine his fighting. He knocked Dickey's cap off and damned near spiked him trying to get to Piersall again. I don't want to be losing any of my coaches."

But Billy had deep reason to regret that fight under the stands in Fenway Park. Just two days later, Piersall was sent down to Birmingham, a Boston farm team.

"It's my fault," said Billy, really troubled. "How could I do something like that? What's the matter with me? I sent him to the minors. I didn't really want anything like that to happen."

But it wasn't Billy Martin's fault. Only a short while later, Piersall was sent from Birmingham to a hospital, suffering from a complete nervous breakdown.

"I'm really ashamed," said Billy. "I just didn't know he was on the verge of a crackup. How could I know?"

It was totally different in Billy's second fight of the season, just four weeks later with Clint Courtney, the same Courtney who had spiked Arky Biggs in Phoenix and put him out of the game for the season. Billy never liked him. If he ever had a real hate, it was for Clint Courtney.

"He didn't know how to fight, he was big and tough and he was crude," said Billy. "In all his actions on the field he played like a deliberately dirty player. He didn't know how to slide. He was awkward. He'd go out of the baseline and jump into the second baseman or the shortstop."

Billy's feelings about Courtney were intense.

"Down in Phoenix I missed one game and a kid by the name of Eddie Lenne was playing second base and Courtney jumps into him and spikes his leg open. That kid Eddie was a neighbor of mine in Berkeley and we played high school ball together. He got killed in Korea."

Billy Martin fumes just recalling the incident.

"I couldn't get Courtney that day," says Billy. "I was in the stands. But from that day on, every time I got the chance, I took a punch at him. Every time."

The first such chance of 1952 came in a game with the St. Louis Browns at Yankee Stadium.

Courtney had been signed by the Yankees originally before he was traded to the St. Louis club. At the Stadium, obviously to show the Yankee organization that they had made a mistake, Courtney was particularly rough in this initial series between the two teams.

The Yankees discussed Courtney's play in the locker room before the game.

"Someone has to take care of him," Mickey Mantle said.

Billy said, "I'll take care of him!"

He didn't need any urging. And he got his chance before the game was over.

Courtney got in the first lick. In the second inning, he kicked a double-play ball out of Martin's glove. It was different in the eighth.

There were two outs in the St. Louis half, and Courtney was on first.

He tried to steal second base.

Yogi threw a strike to Billy, covering the bag and, as Courtney boomed into second in his usual crude, even brutal style, aiming for a collision with the second baseman, Billy slammed the ball into Courtney's mouth.

Martin cocked his fists. But Courtney was evidently dazed. Billy waited for a moment, but when Courtney failed to attack, he just tossed away his glove and began to walk back to the dugout.

But Courtney got over his shock fast, and he rushed, mad as a bull, for Martin, who had his back turned to him.

"Watch out!" yelled Allie Reynolds. "Duck!"

Billy turned fast and, before Courtney could get in his swing, Billy dropped him with a smash to the jaw.

Courtney, however, was up on his feet quickly and swinging away wildly.

Billy, street-fight wise, knew how to handle the wild swing, and got in a few more licks for Eddie Lenne, Arky Biggs, and himself.

It took the umpires to separate them.

It took Casey Stengel to keep Martin in the game. It was all right to throw out Clint Courtney, but Martin was only defending himself.

"A man's got a right to defend himself," argued Casey, and the umpires were convinced of his wisdom.

"A fellow has to take care of himself," said Billy, explaining his role in the fracas. "He also has to take care of his friends," he added.

With the passing years, Billy Martin began to question himself and his readiness to get into a fight, though his soul-searching didn't seem to slow him down too much.

"I know the Bible says you should turn the other cheek," he said, thoughtfully, "and I think a lot about it. Maybe I'll turn the other cheek off the field, but God couldn't have known much about baseball. In baseball you've got to stand up and fight. Back off and you're finished, through, out of the big leagues in a hurry."

Billy's two fights made him good copy for the New York sportswriters. But it was his outstanding play in the field and his clutch hitting that had the fans cheering for him.

He was the pivot man at second base that set a Yankee team record for double plays, 199. Few base runners dashing into second succeeded in knocking him out of the play. He had established a solid reputation throughout the league, and few base runners had the nerve to challenge him.

At bat, Billy became known as the best .267 hitter in baseball. He was always there with the timely hit that sparked a rally, won a big game. It was Billy's eleventh-inning single against the Athletics late in August that scored two runs and clinched the 1952 pennant for Casey Stengel and the New York Yankees.

He was able to collect but five hits in twenty-three times at bat against the Dodgers in the World Series, but he drove home four runs, and one of his five hits was a home run.

It was on the field that Martin truly proved himself. He thrived on the tough competitive atmosphere on the team and his heady play and hustle were an inspiration to his teammates.

He was able to steal coaching signs from the opposing teams and move his infield around to counter the next move. He became another manager on the playing field.

Andy Pafko was on third base for the Dodgers in the fourth game of the World Series, with the Dodgers one run behind and their pitcher, Joe Black, at the plate.

Billy kept his eyes on Charlie Dressen, the Dodgers' manager, who was coaching at third base. Billy studied the crazy hand moves Dressen was going through as he signaled Black at the plate. Billy suspected Dressen was flashing a squeeze-bunt sign to Black. It was the same sign Dressen had used back when he was the manager at Oakland. Billy looked back at Joe Black, and suddenly he had a hunch the squeeze was on. He yelled to Yankee pitcher Allie Reynolds that there might be a squeeze bunt; Allie nodded and came in with a pitchout to

Yogi Berra. Black vainly tried to hit the ball, and missed. Pafko, who was running with the pitch, was easily tagged out at home.

It was smart, heads-up baseball.

The greatest play Billy made, however, came in the seventh inning of the seventh and deciding game of the 1952 World Series.

The Dodgers were behind, 4–2, but, with two out, the bases were loaded and the always dangerous Jackie Robinson was up at bat.

With the count three and two, the three Dodger base runners—Carl Furillo, Billy Cox, and Pee Wee Reese, were off and streaking as Jackie hit a very high pop fly that should have been an easy out for Joe Collins at first base. It wasn't.

The ball was up high in the afternoon sun and Collins lost the ball in the sun. Bob Kuzava, the Yankee pitcher, got as far from the ball as he could. Berra kept yelling at Collins to go get the ball, but Collins was frozen in his tracks. Furillo had crossed the plate. So had Billy Cox. They waved frantically for Reese, who had already reached third, to come on home. It was Billy Martin who saved the day.

Billy recalled the play recently and explains it this way: "It was a three-and-two count on Jackie Robinson and I played him to pull the ball, moving closer to second base, and I was almost on the outfield grass. When the ball went up in the air I looked at Collins and I saw that Joe had lost the ball in the sun. We'd been having trouble with the sun all day. I took off. I was worried about the wind because the prevailing wind at Ebbets Field blew the ball toward home plate. Also I was thinking about Yogi. I was afraid he'd be coming out for the ball, and sometimes when he did he kept his mask on. I heard nothing, no one yelling, no one calling me off the ball. But I knew I might run into somebody. So when I reached down and grabbed the ball with my glove, I pulled it out and held it in my bare hand. If you get knocked out, you'll squeeze the ball in your glove for some reason. But I didn't run into anybody and I didn't think the play was so much until I got back to the dugout and they were all slapping me on the back and saying 'Great play!' I was really surprised. But later, when I saw the films of the play, I realized how far I had run for the ball. It was a good play."

It was a game-saving catch. It was the World Series-saving catch. Kuzava kept the Dodgers from scoring in the eighth and ninth, and the Yankees were once again the world champions.

Billy Martin was a hero.

For Casey, it was his fourth World Series championship in a row, a feat no other manager in the game except Joe McCarthy of the same Yankees had to his credit.

For Billy Martin it meant an endless number of off-season banquets, with the Kid as the guest speaker; and Billy loved it all. He appeared as guest speaker at dozens of banquets and dinners, and he thoroughly enjoyed the limelight and the adulation. That winter of 1952, Billy Martin was in all his glory and the music was all for him, all but one bitter note.

Lois, his young wife, was pregnant. With Billy gone, away all spring and summer, playing baseball, then off on the banquet circuit most of the winter, she was alone and unhappy. Berkeley was all right, but she didn't enjoy being home alone.

Just about a couple of weeks after she was delivered of her baby, Kelly Ann, she woke Billy, who had been sleeping late after a big night out, alone.

"There's a man at the door who wants to see you," she said.

"Can't you get it?" he asked, turning his face to the wall.

"No," said Lois. "He wants to see you."

Billy got out of bed, mumbled something unintelligible, and opened the door.

"Mr. Martin?" said a complete stranger.

"Yeah, I'm Mr. Martin. What do you want?"

"I've got something for you," said the stranger, and he handed him a sheaf of legal documents.

Lois was suing him for a divorce.

"You can't stay in love with a newspaper clipping, not for long, not forever."

Billy tried arguing, battling.

"I fought it out of love, pride, hurt," Billy said.

He fought it because he wanted and needed to be loved. He fought it because the one thing the rough-and-tough Billy Martin couldn't take was rejection.

It was rejection that almost destroyed him in 1953.

CHAPTER NINE

Best Year

EVERYTHING LOOKED BRIGHT FOR THE YANKEES IN THE SPRING OF 1953, when Casey Stengel called his young team together at St. Petersburg, Florida. Mickey Mantle was soon smashing the ball great distances. Whitey Ford was back from a tour with the Army. Yogi Berra had developed into the best catcher in the league, and little Phil Rizzuto was without a peer at short. With Gene Woodling, Hank Bauer, or Irv Noren flanking Mantle, theirs was a tremendous outfield. Vic Raschi and Allie Reynolds still held the peak in pitching, while Eddie Lopat was driving the batters to distraction with his slow stuff.

"Lopat," Casey said, "looks like he is throwing wads of tissue paper. Every time he wins a game, fans come down out of the stands asking for contracts. They say if he can get the batters out, they can. But it ain't as easy as it looks."

Johnny Sain and Tom Gorman were the relief pitchers, with an occasional lift from Ewell Blackwell, claimed from the Reds the year before. McDougald was the regular third baseman. Another youngster, from that great reservoir of Yankee talent, the Bay Area of San Francisco, was a utility infielder named Andy Carey. Johnny Mize, although slowed to a walk, could still hit the ball a mile, and he once again shared first base with Joe Collins.

Spring training in 1953 should have been the best of times for young Billy Martin. He had completely recovered from his broken ankle of a year ago and was assured of his job at second base. But he was an extremely unhappy young man. He was tense, nervous, and jittery.

"The guys who are happy playing ball are those who can adjust to the nuthouse they have to live in," he said.

There's a nuthouse quality to the game, all right, but Martin's nuthouse wasn't baseball; it was his own private life, and his own private life was a mess.

He had tried to effect a reconciliation with his wife, Lois, who had served him with official separation papers a few months previously, and he would continue to make every effort he could to save his marriage, but Lois wasn't to be moved. She wanted the divorce and she was adamant about it.

Billy took to sleeping pills; they didn't help.

"Most nights I'd been walking the floor until sunlight," he said.

He was depressed, and as the race for the pennant heightened, his depression got worse. He had always gone to Sunday Mass; he began to go to Mass at St. Patrick's Cathedral every morning when the Yankees were in New York. He said his rosary every night. He became jittery. His depression deepened. He was on the verge of a complete mental breakdown.

He constantly called Lois on the telephone, telling her how much he loved her, pleading with her to change her mind about the divorce, if only for their child's sake. Sometimes Lois was pleasant enough on the phone. More often she just hung up on him.

"I don't love you anymore."

Mickey Mantle, happily married and with a child of his own, could understand the turmoil that had Billy Martin in a vise; they were rooming together now, and Mickey was witness to all of Billy's distress, but there was little he could do about it. Mickey tried. He would wrestle with him, play tricks, joke with him in the dressing room, on the field, back in their room, anything; get him to go out to dinner with Whitey Ford. Mickey was Billy's best friend, but there was no way he could give Billy Martin the peace of mind he needed so badly.

Ironically, 1953 was Billy Martin's greatest year as a professional ballplayer.

It was the year, too, in which Whitey Ford came out of the service to rejoin the Yankees, to become, with Mickey Mantle

and Billy Martin, one of The Terrible Trio, the hell-raising
Yankee version of The Three Musketeers.

He was christened Edward Charles Ford, and it was the old
Yankee pitching star, Lefty Gomez, who first called him
Whitey. He was born on East Sixty-sixth Street in Manhattan,
and he grew up across the East River in Astoria. He fought
with the other kids in the streets, played ball on the empty lots,
chased fire engines, played hookey from school, and ran from
the cops. He shakes his head when he is asked what he wanted
to be when he grew up. A fireman? A cop? A prizefighter? A
ballplayer?

"I don't know," he said. "I never thought much about it.
Baseball was my favorite game, but I never said to myself I was
going to be a big-leaguer."

As a youngster, Ed "Whitey" Ford had reason to be excited.
He was small and he was left-handed, both of which worked
against him. In Astoria, the Thirty-fourth Avenue Boys were a
first-rate team, and if Ford had been right-handed he might
have made the club easily as an infielder. If he had been
bigger, he would have been offered first base. But as things
were, he had to struggle. When he was young, older, stronger
boys pitched. Ford didn't want to play the outfield. So he
battled, and since he could hit, hustle, and was aggressive, he
became the best five-foot, four-inch first baseman the Thirty-
fourth Avenue Boys ever had.

Like his friends on the team, Ford was tough: not in the
sense that boys can be tough now with knives and guns, but
tough in an unpretentious way.

He was a New York subway kid. He thought a good cheap
way to kill time was to take a long subway ride. Once when he
was playing for the Thirty-fourth Avenue Boys and Billy Loes
was pitching for the Astoria Cubs, the two future big-league
stars took the BMT subway from Astoria to Coney Island, a
ride of perhaps an hour and a half. They stayed on the train
until it turned around and came back to Astoria. It was one
way to stretch a nickel in New York some thirty-five years ago.

When Ford graduated from elementary school, he might have enrolled at Bryant High School near his home, just as Billy Loes did. But his best friend, Johnny Martin, who was a fine catcher, talked him into entering Manhattan High School of Aviation Trades, where the two could learn to become airplane mechanics.

At the first baseball tryout at Manhattan Aviation, Martin locked up the catching position. But Ford was troubled. The team already had a fine first baseman.

"Why don't you try pitching?" Martin said. "Those pitchers don't look like much. You can throw better than any of them."

Ford respected Martin's baseball judgment. "Okay," he said.

After a successful high school career that included six straight victories in one season and a 1–0 loss in the championship game, Ford wrote to the Yankees for a tryout.

He applied as a first baseman. By this time he had grown to five-seven, and of course he got no serious consideration. But the late Paul Kritchell, the most successful baseball scout of all time, saw something in the way Ford threw.

"Stop thinking about first base," Kritchell said. "Think about pitching, and I'll see you in a couple of years."

A month later in September the Thirty-fourth Avenue Boys met the Bay Ridge Cubs of Brooklyn for the city championship at the Polo Grounds.

Lou DeAngelis, the Bay Ridge pitcher, threw a no-hitter at Astoria for ten innings. Then Ford led off the eleventh with a double and scored on another hit. He then struck out three straight Cubs to wrap up a thrilling 1–0 victory, then hurried to the clubhouse ready to talk to all the baseball scouts. An hour later, bitterly disappointed when no scouts appeared, he took the subway back home to Astoria.

Two days later the Dodgers telephoned and offered Ford a three-thousand-dollar bonus. The Giants called and went to four thousand dollars. After a week of bidding, he signed with the Yankees for a seven-thousand-dollar bonus.

In the spring of 1947 Ford was sent to Binghamton for

spring training. He was there a month and then was shipped down to Butler in the Class C Middle Atlantic League, by manager Lefty Gomez. Whitey won thirteen games at Butler, and then at Norfolk in the Class B Piedmont League in 1948, he won sixteen games while losing eight.

Ford spent three years in the minors, pitching impressively and moving up the minor-league ladder each year, completing a 16–5 record for Binghamton in the Class A Eastern League in 1949.

Toward the end of the season, as the Yankees were battling furiously to beat out Boston for the pennant, Whitey telephoned Casey Stengel to let him know he could help the Yankees beat Boston.

"Bring me up, Casey. Give me the ball, and I'll deliver the Red Sox to you."

Casey turned down the generous offer, but later he said he should have listened to the brash youngster.

"I bet he would have done just what he said he would do."

In his first game as a Yankee, in 1950, he turned to Casey, just before he walked to the mound, and said, like a cock crowing, "OK, Case. You just sit back and watch. You've got nothing to worry about."

Whitey gave Casey very little to worry about, pitching for the Yanks. He gave him a lot to worry about off the field, with his buddies, Mickey Mantle and Billy Martin, The Three Musketeers.

Casey didn't worry about their capers in the locker room of the Stadium, it wasn't their running around the dressing room, half naked, sometimes completely naked, shooting cap guns and water pistols at each other, to see which man was the quickest on the draw; it was their nighttime activities in restaurants, nightclubs, and more often in the bars that troubled the old man. And one of those capers was eventually to prove disastrous for the three happy-go-lucky ballplayers.

Strangely enough, it was Billy Martin who took the blame for most of their capers. As far as George Weiss was concerned, Billy Martin was the team troublemaker, leading Ford and Mantle into all kinds of escapades.

"That wasn't the case at all," says Whitey, recalling a few of the good times. Billy got blamed for a lot of things he never did.

"One time we were in Chicago," said Whitey, "and we went to this Polynesian restaurant. The waiter said he would only give us two zombies each, so naturally we decided to have three. And Billy convinced him to give us three. I think there were seven ounces of rum in each one of them. And after we finished the third one, we looked at our watches, and it was late, and we had to catch a train to the next city. We must have run about five blocks to the train station. It was a real hot night and when we got there, we were soaking wet. And then Mickey and Billy got into a wrestling match. The two of them used to wrestle all the time. And we got on the train, and the next thing you know the two of them were throwing up all over the train.

"Another time," said Whitey, "the three of us went on a hunting trip. We were in Kerrville, Texas, and we had an old 1930 Model-T convertible, and we were chugging along when we spotted a deer. I was sitting in the rumble seat, and Mickey and Billy were in the front seat. We saw the deer, and they both jumped out of the car in front of me, they were about five feet apart, Billy on my left, Mickey on my right, and I stayed in my seat, and I fired my gun right between them. Pow! I aimed and shot right between their heads. They hit the dirt, face first in opposite directions, like you see the guys do in war movies. They turned sheet white. Every time I think about that hunting trip, I shudder," Whitey said. "I almost wiped out the Yankee team.

"Matter of fact," said Whitey, "Mickey and I used to tease the hell out of Billy, kid him that he was leading us astray. But that wasn't the case, 'cause Billy really didn't drink that much. He wasn't what you call a real drinker. But he'd go out with us, nurse a drink all night. I caught him once tossing his drinks into a flower pot.

" 'What did you do with your drink?' I asked him.

" 'I drank it,' Billy said.

" 'Oh yeah! Well, where's the ice in your glass? You dumped it, you phony.' "

Whitey Ford is a wealthy man today. He has invested wisely in real estate and in the stock market, and has done several television commercials with his pal Mickey Mantle.

Whitey was one of the all-time Yankee pitching stars, but above all, he was and is today a likable and unassuming regular guy.

"I don't like to be made a big thing of," Ford once said.

"I just like to go someplace, and you buy one, and I buy one."

Whitey Ford came out of the service just in time to join the team for the opening game of the 1953 season. He came just in time to see Mickey Mantle hit one of the longest home runs in history in the opening game against Washington. Mantle hit a towering home run over the left-field bleachers in Washington's Griffith Stadium that carried some 565 feet. Gene Woodling began to terrorize enemy pitchers, and Billy Martin clouted the ball and played magnificently at second base as the Yankees moved past the Cleveland Indians to go into first place.

There was a tension-filled game with the St. Louis Browns on April 25, when the Yankees defeated the Browns in ten innings. Mantle homered, and there was a fierce free-for-all battle at the finish. Scoring the winning run, McDougald crashed into the Browns' catcher, Clint Courtney, bowling him over. In the home half of the inning Courtney retaliated by crashing into little Phil Rizzuto at second base, spiking him badly in the right leg. Both benches erupted and were battling each other all over the field, but Billy Martin beat everybody to Courtney and bloodied his face and battered him with a series of smashing lefts and rights to Clint's jaw. For good measure, Yankee outfielder Bob Cerv stomped Courtney's glasses. An angry mob waited outside the park when the game was over, and the Yankees' bus had an escort of two police cars on its journey back to the Chase Hotel.

A couple of days later, in Detroit, catcher Matt Batts of the Tigers put out Martin at the plate as Billy attempted to score. Batts slammed the ball into Billy's mouth and knocked him down, but in a flash Billy was up and exchanging furious punches with Batts until they were separated.

Boos were becoming familiar to Martin. "I was hooted, booed in about every city in the league," Billy said after retiring as an active player. "Not just by a few baseball nuts, either. It seemed like everyone in the park was down on me. Then, after the ball game was over, I'd get to feeling awful bad, but I had no home, no one to share my misery with."

By the first week in June the Yankees had a five-and-one-half-game lead over Cleveland. The Yankees took a winning streak into the West and ran up eighteen wins in a row and an eleven-game lead over the Indians. Then came a leveling-off period in which everything seemed to go wrong. The Yankees lost nine games in a row and their lead dropped to four games. Mickey Mantle was out with a badly twisted knee, Mize was hurting too, and it was Billy Martin who broke through that pall of gloom in a squeaker of a game against the Boston Red Sox when it looked like the Yanks were going to lose No. 10 in a row. In the ninth inning Mize pinch-hit and cracked out a long two-base hit. Martin promptly sent Johnny home with a clutch single to win the game for the Yankees and put an end to the lengthy nine-game losing streak.

Shortly thereafter, on September 14, on homers by Berra and Martin, and good relief pitching by Johnny Sain, the Yankees defeated the Indians to win the pennant for the fifth time in a row.

As the 1953 season drew to a close, Martin's emotional state was in a crisis. "I was about to crack up mentally before the Series," he once admitted.

Billy didn't look like he was going to crack up at the champagne party in the clubhouse following the 1953 pennant victory. Nor did he seem to be especially tense in the Latin Quarter, one of New York's top night spots at the time, laughing it up with his two pals, Whitey Ford and Mickey Mantle, and a couple of other Yankees who joined them for the extended celebration. When the bill came at the end of the evening, Billy offered to pay the whole tab.

Whitey Ford looked at the bill.

"Two hundred fifty bucks. Say we all chip in."

Everybody in the party was willing, but the cash wasn't there among all of them.

"I've got a better idea," said Whitey.

He laid the bill on the table and signed it "Dan Topping."

Dan Topping, co-owner of the Yankees, was celebrating in the Latin Quarter that night, too.

Then for good measure, Whitey signed his own name to the bill, along with Mickey Mantle's and Billy Martin's.

"I don't think this is going to get us into any trouble," said Whitey to the other Yankees with them, "but we'll leave your names out. We'll play it safe."

Dan Topping didn't see the humor in it.

"I don't think this is funny at all!" he snapped at the three stars. "It's going to cost each of you five hundred dollars off your paychecks!"

At a victory party just a couple of weeks later, Billy and Mickey cornered Dan Topping, and Billy did a con job on Dan, which Billy could do with the best of them.

"That five-hundred-dollar fine, Mr. Topping," he said. "Wasn't that a bit steep? We were all celebrating the same thing. It was a great win, wasn't it? And we were just having a little fun. We never expected you to pay the bill. You know that, don't you?"

Dan Topping grinned. He was too happy, celebrating the record wins of his New York club, to keep a straight face.

"OK," he said. "But never again!"

And he took his checkbook out of his pocket and wrote each of them a check for five hundred dollars.

The two boys then scouted around for Whitey and showed him their checks.

"Go over and ask Topping for yours," said Billy.

"Tell him to stick it up his ass," said Whitey.

Whitey, the kid out of New York City, was probably the toughest of the trio.

Still, for all the partying and celebrating, for all the pranks, Billy Martin would say, later, "I was just about ready for the straitjacket going into the 1953 World Series."

No one looking at him play and hit in that Series could have possibly guessed the stress and strain under which the ballplayer lived and operated.

Billy Martin played his heart out, or his venom, his love, his anger, or all of them, and delivered the greatest performance in his professional career as a ballplayer.

In later years Casey Stengel rated his 1953 Yankees as the finest team he ever managed. He singled out four of his players. "We got the best shortstop in baseball in Phil Rizzuto," he said, "the best hustling-fighting second baseman in Billy Martin. Yogi is the best catcher in this game today, and Mickey Mantle the best center fielder, and the pitching can't be beat."

In the World Series that fall the Yankees faced the Brooklyn Dodgers, possibly the finest aggregation of all-stars one team ever fielded. Roy Campanella, one of baseball's all-time catchers, was the mainstay behind the plate. In Duke Snider and Carl Furillo, who was the National League's batting champion with a .344 average, the Dodgers had the finest one-two punch in baseball. First baseman Gil Hodges hit 31 home runs and was a fine defensive man at first. The great Jackie Robinson was in left field, Pee Wee Reese, one of baseball's finest, was at short; Billy Cox, a solid defensive man, was at third; and Junior Gilliam was the Rookie of the Year at second base.

In the first inning of the first game, at Yankee Stadium, Billy Martin came up to hit against the great curve-ball star Carl Erskine. The Yankees were leading, 1–0. The bases were loaded, and Martin, on the first pitch, drove a tremendous triple over Jackie Robinson's head in left field as three Yankees came home to score. Martin's triple drove Erskine from the box, and the Yankees went on to win, 9–5.

In the second game, against Preacher Roe, with the Dodgers

leading, 2–1, Martin waited on a fast ball, and then drove the pitch into the stands for a home run that tied the score. Mickey Mantle delivered the big punch in the eighth inning, a two-run homer that won the game for the Yankees.

The Dodgers won the third game, at Brooklyn.

In the fourth game, Roy Campanella slammed the ball hard into Martin's face as Billy came sliding into home after Mantle singled him in from second base. Billy was up fast with his fists clenched and ready for action. But for once in his life he controlled his temper, and it was just as well, for Campanella was as tough a scrapper as Billy and some fifty pounds heavier. Earlier Billy smashed a long three-base hit off the delivery of Billy Loes, but the Dodgers won the game, 7–3.

In the fifth game Billy slammed a two-run homer off Russ Meyer as the Yankees won, 11–7.

The sixth game was a tense and thrilling battle that will doubtless be remembered as long as baseball is played. Chuck Dressen started Carl Erskine, who set a record in the third game by striking out fourteen Yankees at Ebbets Field. But Carl, with only two days' rest, was blasted for three runs in the first two innings as Whitey Ford held the Dodgers scoreless until the sixth inning when Jackie Robinson doubled, stole third, and scored on a deep drive to center field to make the score 3–1.

Actually, all the drama began in the eighth inning, when Casey, in a move as startling as any in his career, withdrew Whitey Ford and came in with Allie Reynolds.

The Chief, who had started the opening game, had strained a muscle in his back in that game. However, he came back to stop the threatening Dodgers in the ninth inning of the fifth game. Now Casey called on him to lock up the final game.

Ford, in the seven innings he pitched, had given the Dodgers only six hits. He was leading, 3–1, and there seemed to be no apparent reason for making a change, but Casey wanted Reynolds. And so Allie Reynolds came in to pitch to Jackie Robinson, and Jackie promptly singled to left. But Reynolds, calling on all of his great firepower, got two out and then a big third out by striking out the always dangerous Roy Campanella to end the inning.

Gil Hodges, first up for the Brooks in the ninth flied out. Big Duke Snider worked Reynolds carefully, refusing to hit Allie's big curve, and Allie walked him.

Then Carl Furillo stepped up to the plate. He watched carefully, patiently, and worked the count to three and two. Then he smashed a Reynolds fast ball into the lower right-field stands to tie the score at 3–3 as the Flatbush faithful went absolutely crazy in the stands. Allie then turned on all of his vaunted firepower to strike out Billy Cox and Clem Labine to end the inning.

Hank Bauer walked in the last of the ninth inning.

Yogi Berra flied out, but Mickey Mantle topped a ball that skipped off Billy Cox's glove at third and was given a hit.

Now the stage was set for a dramatic climax as Billy Martin stepped in to hit. Martin, clearly the Series hero to this point, had tripled in the first game with the bases loaded, had hit two homers, and up to this moment he had eleven hits, tops for the Series.

Clem Labine worked carefully on the mound for the Brooks, got the count to one and one. Then Billy drove the next pitch right over second base to score Hank Bauer with the winning run, to clinch the record-breaking fifth straight World Series for Casey Stengel and his Yankees.

Billy, who never hit more than .270 in the major leagues, hit .500 in the Series. His 12 hits included 7 singles, a double, 2 triples, and 2 homers. His 23 total bases broke Babe Ruth's record of 19 for a 6-game Series.

Billy Martin had been the hero in the 1952 Series with his timely hitting and his incredible catch of Jackie Robinson's pop fly over the pitcher's mound. Now he was the hero, acclaimed by all. In the locker room immediately following the game, Stengel, Yankee owners Dan Topping and Del Webb, and all Billy's fellow teammates almost crushed him with their embraces. It was the greatest moment in the life of Billy Martin, who says he was born to be a Yankee.

"That's the worst thing that could have happened to Martin," said Casey Stengel, with a bit of his tongue in his cheek. "I ain't going to be able to live with that little son-of-a-bitch next year."

But Casey wouldn't have to "live with that little son-of-a-bitch next year." In 1954, the United States Army would have to live with Billy.

CHAPTER TEN

The Yankees Lose
the Championship

BILLY MARTIN GOT A HERO'S WELCOME WHEN HE RETURNED TO
West Berkeley after the 1953 World Series. And the Oakland
fans gave him a gala dinner party and as a gift a baby-blue
Cadillac to show their appreciation for the hometown boy who
made good. He had already received a Packard for winning the
Most Valuable Player award in the World Series, and he very
graciously drove the car over to his old pastor, Father Dennis
Moore, and presented the car to him as a token of appreciation
for the kindness Father Moore had shown when the Martin
family needed help.

The first thing Billy did, however, on getting back to the
Bay Area was to visit with his wife, Lois. He did everything he
possibly could to try to patch up their differences. He failed.
He never got her to change her mind, and their divorce became final at the end of the year.

Failing to get Lois to change her mind, he went home and
did not move out of his mother's house for an entire week. He
spent most of the week sleeping, and just sitting about the
house. He was exhausted, emotionally and physically; especially
emotionally. He could have cashed in on the quick fame he
got for his performance in the World Series, but he turned
down all the personal-appearance offers that came his way. He
was completely worn to a frazzle and just wanted to rest and
relax.

Then it was off to Commerce, Oklahoma, to go fishing and
hunting with his pal, Mickey Mantle. The front office had gotten wind of Billy's intention to join Mickey for the winter, and
had sent out numerous signals to indicate that they didn't ap-
prove. They were afraid that Billy was going to corrupt their

ace slugger, which Billy could never do, and would never want to do.

Billy didn't even bother to acknowledge the front-office signals. He ate quail and mashed potatoes with Mickey for breakfast, fished and hunted with him throughout most of the winter, and relaxed enough to put on some twenty pounds and to lose much of his tension and jitters.

One day Billy called New York columnist Jimmy Cannon on the phone and said he was playing basketball on a team that was coached by Mickey Mantle. "He's a lousy coach," said Billy. "Every time I score a basket he pulls me out of the game."

Back in Berkeley meanwhile, several people who for one reason or another didn't like Billy Martin particularly, wrote to his draft board. The substance of those letters was: "We know all about Mr. Martin's hardship discharge back in 1950, after a few weeks with the Army, but how do you give a hardship discharge to a man who is earning about fifteen thousand dollars a year playing for the New York Yankees and who just received more than eight thousand dollars for playing in the World Series?"

The draft board reconsidered that hardship discharge and in March of 1954, just before the Yankees began to assemble for spring training, and just about two months before Billy reached his twenty-sixth birthday, at which time he could no longer be drafted, he received notice of his reclassification —1-A.

Billy Martin's reaction to the notification was calm enough.

"I'd rather play ball," he said, "but I'm still young and it's not going to ruin me. And what the hell, I can't beef. I got Jerry Coleman's job when the Marines took him, didn't I?"

But then he had second thoughts. He still had to support Lois and his baby daughter, in addition to his mother, his asthmatic stepfather, and his sister.

"I'll be glad to go into the Army," he said, "if they can figure some way I can support all those people depending on me."

He appealed his reclassification.

"Is that car yours?" asked one member of the draft board at the hearing that was called to decide the validity of the 1-A classification.

"Yeah," said Billy. "You must have read about it in the papers."

"If you're having all that trouble supporting your family, why don't you sell it? Give the money to your dependents?"

"For how long will that keep them in potatoes?" Billy queried.

They didn't bother to answer. His reclassification stood. The draft board put him at the top of the draft list.

Much of the board's decision must be laid at the doors of the San Francisco and Berkeley newspapers, his own Bay Area newspapers. More than three hundred letters attacking Billy for selfishness and lack of patriotism reached just one of the number of San Francisco newspapers. Berkeley newspapers attacked Billy for the same reasons, editorially.

Whatever the justice of the case, and wherever justice lay, Billy Martin was drafted almost immediately and spent the next seventeen months in the Army, at Fort Carson, Colorado.

He was a good soldier. He became a corporal. To the astonishment of his good friends Mickey Mantle and Whitey Ford, not to speak of his countless friends and enemies in the baseball world, he won a good-conduct medal. He had his first chance at managing, while in the Army, as player-manager of the championship post team.

While he was at camp, there was a congressional investigation of charges that the Army was coddling its athletes. Martin didn't think he was being coddled. He knew he wasn't being coddled. He wrote an emotional letter to Congressman William E. Hess of Ohio, who was heading the investigation.

"If I'm being coddled," he wrote, "so was General Jonathan Wainwright after Corregidor."

General Wainwright was in the Death March that the Japanese forced on their American prisoners on Bataan.

The letter caused a stir in the press; none of it was favorable to Billy Martin.

Mickey Mantle hurriedly flew out to Fort Carson to plead with Billy to shut up and stop his letter-writing campaign. But the storm over Billy's head soon subsided and he was discharged from the Army in August 1955. Physically, he was in the best condition of his life, and he had finally come to terms with his separation from Lois and his child. But there were other things that had disturbed and upset him while he was in the service.

He had followed the fortunes of the Yankees throughout the 1954 baseball season, rooted for them, and suffered a deep disappointment when the Yankees failed in their battle for a sixth straight championship. Without Billy, it was the first time in five seasons the Yankees had lost the American League flag. He was sure the pennant, and the World Series too, would have been theirs, if he had been playing second base in his Yankee uniform. Instead, he had been wearing the Army drab, and somehow he felt it was his fault that the Yankees hadn't made it to the top.

He had the same feelings as he read about the Yankees' fortunes in 1955. The Cleveland Indians, the Chicago White Sox, the Boston Red Sox, and the New York club, each in turn, forged to the front in the race for the flag, then fell behind. It was one of the tightest pennant races in years, and Billy felt he would have made the difference, that he could have propelled the Yankees in front to stay.

And the baseball scene revived much of his antagonism for the draft board.

"I'm sore," he said. "If they threw me out of the Army because I had five dependents, why did they put me back in again with five dependents? Because I got my name in the papers? They didn't have the guts to stand up against all those cranks who are always after my blood. I'm glad to serve my country, but why did they leave me out the first time?"

There was another reason why Billy Martin was angry.

"I'm twenty-seven years old and I've nothing in the world but my name and my daughter."

In time he would lose his daughter. He couldn't forget that he was broke, and he would let his teammates on the New York club know about it in short order.

When Billy returned in early September 1955, Mickey Mantle was there of course to welcome the returning Yankee to the fold. So was Whitey Ford. But no one was happier to see him back in the Yankee uniform than his old manager, Casey Stengel.

Defending Billy against the front office, back in 1953, Casey made a speech for Martin that summed up his evaluation of the ballplayer, man and boy.

"He's a real good ballplayer," said Case, who may have had a peculiar way of making a point, but made it anyway. "And I don't mean that he can field, throw, run bases, hit, make the double play, and win ball games," he went on. "I also mean he is good for the manager, good for the owners.

"Now I wish the owners would realize this," he added for good measure, "and quit bothering me about the Kid.

"That fresh little bastard. How I love him."

The old codger all but kissed Martin on his return from the Army, and he had good reason to rejoice. Not only was Casey getting the vital sparkplug for the club, he also was getting back the boy who, for all purposes, was his son.

"You don't beat Stengel when he's got Billy Martin," wrote sportswriter Bill Corum in the old *Journal-American*.

Billy said to Casey, "Case, when we were bushers out in Oakland, we played on a winner. And when we came to New York, we never played on anything but winners. Take my word for it, there's nothing to worry about. We'll take this league apart before the end of the season."

His first game, late in that 1955 season, was on the second of September; and there he was hollering and hustling as if he'd never been out of uniform. Whitey Ford pitched a one-hitter against the Washington Senators, Mickey Mantle walloped a three-run homer to win the game, and quite suddenly the pennant race began to wind down as three clubs—Cleveland, Chicago, and the Yankees—battled to stay in front.

A number of the old stars had departed from Yankee Stadium when Billy Martin made his dramatic return, the great pitchers Vic Raschi and Allie Reynolds, and Bob Kuzava and Gene Woodling, among others. There were new faces, too: Bob Turley, Don Larsen, the young Bob Grim, a twenty-game winner and winner of the Rookie of the Year award in 1954; Bill (Moose) Skowron and Country Slaughter; and Elston Howard, the first black man to play ball in a Yankee uniform, and to make baseball history for the Yankee organization.

Martin was once more the spark of the team. He hollered, he scrambled, and he fired up everybody on the team, and they began to win.

On September 2, the Yankees found themselves two full games behind the Cleveland Indians.

A team meeting was held and Billy was the speaker and he was angry.

"I had three cars when I went into the Army," he shouted at his teammates in a clubhouse meeting. "Now I don't even have one. I'm broke! I'm broke and you're playing as though you're trying to lose! We've got to get into the Series! We've got to!"

The veteran Yankees felt the sting and the rookies looked at him with amazement, if not with a bit of awe. Whatever the reason, Martin's very presence ignited the Yankees, and with Yogi Berra having one of his greatest years, the Yanks moved into first place with but ten days to go and held the lead to win yet another pennant for Casey Stengel.

And Billy Martin, the holler guy, the take-charge guy, contributed more than his voice to that sparkling finish in 1955; almost two years out of baseball and fresh out of the Army, he hit for an average of .300 and provided the vital spark the Yankees needed to win the pennant once more.

Once again, the Dodgers and the Yankees clashed in the battle for the world championship. It was a classic series that wasn't decided until the dramatic seventh game of the Series, and by an impossible catch by Sandy Amoros of the Dodgers.

The Yanks, with Whitey Ford and Tommy Byrne pitching, took the first two games in the Stadium. The Dodgers, with Johnny Podres pitching and Roy Campanella hitting, took the

Academy Award winner and Tiger fan George C. Scott and wife Tricia walk with Detroit manager Billy Martin and the hard-hitting Norm Cash at the Tigers' 1973 spring training camp in Lakeland, Florida. Scott arrived wearing the Tigers baseball cap.

October 4, 1972. Billy Martin, manager of the American League's Eastern Division champion Detroit Tigers, had his contract extended through the 1974 baseball season. (*A.P. Photo*)

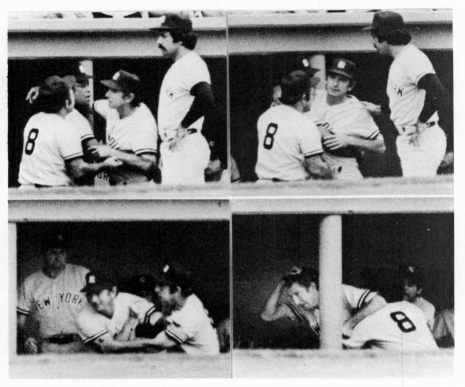

June 18, 1977, Boston Massachusetts. Newspaper photos of Yankees manager Billy Martin being restrained in the dugout in Boston during the game against the Red Sox. Coaches Yogi Berra and Elston Howard hold Martin as he tries to get at Reggie Jackson, not shown in this sequence. Billy pulled Jackson out of the game in the sixth inning, when he loped after a fly ball hit into his area. Billy accused Reggie of not hustling and then lazily throwing the ball to second base.

October 1976. Billy Martin lines up a putt at the Palmas del Mar resort in Puerto Rico after the World Series. (*A.P. photo*)

August 1978. Former and soon-to-be Yankees manager relaxes at Sun Valley in the Danny Thompson Memorial Golf Tournament. Paired with Billy is John Phillips of Fremont, California. (*A.P. photo*)

third game; and Roger Craig, with the help of Clem Labine, held the Yanks at bay in the fifth game, to make it a sweep for the Dodgers in Ebbets Field (the Dodgers had won the fourth game, 8–5).

Whitey Ford kept the Yankees back in the Series with a four-hit pitching performance. Then came the seventh game and an incredible game-saving catch by the Dodgers' Sandy Amoros in the sixth inning of one of the more exciting World Series games.

Johnny Podres was pitching for the Dodgers and he seemed to have nothing on the ball. At least that's the way the Yankees saw it. Yet Johnny had the great Yankee sluggers popping the ball into the air for harmless outs.

"We can beat this guy. He has nothing," was the chorus on the bench, but for five innings Podres had the Yanks blanked.

In the sixth, Billy Martin led off and worked the pitcher for a walk. Gil McDougald followed with a single, Martin stopping at second.

Yogi Berra and his big bat were up at the plate.

With the Dodgers leading, 2–0, and Podres breezing through the Yankee lineup, the New York fans had had little to cheer about. Now they began to whoop it up.

"Come on, Yogi!"

"We wanna hit, Yogi!"

Yogi, intense as always at the plate, was looking for a change-up, but Johnny Podres delivered a fast ball on the outside. Yogi swung late and lined the ball arching high toward the left-field foul pole.

The crowd was on its feet. As the ball left the bat on a line out to left field, the wind lifted it higher and higher. It looked like a home run, or at the very least a ground-rule double. Martin was sure to score; if it cleared the wall, there would be three Yankees home and the Yanks would have the lead.

No one, but no one counted on Sandy Amoros from Matanzas, Cuba, the Dodger import who couldn't speak English but certainly knew how to cover left field.

With the crack of the bat, Sandy was off on a dead run and,

just as he reached the wall, he reached into the stands and grabbed the ball.

Everyone in the stands, except Amoros, was stunned. Sandy then pivoted and whipped the ball to Pee Wee Reese; Pee Wee fired the ball on one hop to Gil Hodges, and Hodges tagged first base before Gil McDougald could get back to it. The inning, which might have turned the entire game around and given the Yankees the win and the championship, was over.

Podres had scattered eight hits, blanked the Yankees, and the Dodgers were the 1955 world champions.

With the last Yankee out, an Ellie Howard two-hopper to Reese and an easy toss to first baseman Gil Hodges, Billy Martin raced into the locker room in tears.

Bill Martin hated defeat, and he had nothing but defeat in the past two years. There was Lois rejecting all his efforts for reconciliation; there was the divorce; there was the unseemly separation from the game he loved, the seventeen months in the Army. And now losing the Series to the Dodgers.

He burst into the locker room. He banged his fists against the lockers, cutting up his fists. Then he hid himself in the trainer's room for an hour. He didn't want anyone to see him with the tears running down his face.

"We should have won," he said to Mickey Mantle later, his eyes still wet with tears.

But, strange as it may seem, and certainly evidence of the complicated character of Martin, Billy was not crying for himself, he was crying for all the team and for all the defeats in his young life.

"We should have won," he said to Mickey Mantle. "It isn't right for a man like Casey to lose."

Billy blamed himself.

"I should have hit Johnny Podres, especially in the late innings," he said. "Podres was giving me the change-up all day. I should have known he'd feed me fast balls with the light getting bad. I just didn't think."

Billy was one of the brightest Yankee stars in that World Series. He got eight hits, batted .320, and drove in four runs.

It wasn't enough for Billy.

"It's a shame for a man like Casey to lose."

Old Casey loved "the little bastard."

Billy Martin loved the old rascal.

CHAPTER ELEVEN

High Times in Japan

A COUPLE OF WEEKS AFTER THE LOSS IN THE 1955 WORLD Series, the entire Yankee ball club, with the sole exception of Phil Rizzuto, took off on a jaunt across the Pacific. The first stop was the Hawaiian Islands for a couple of weeks, then a week more in Wake Island, the Philippines, and Guam. The tour would end in Japan, where they were scheduled to play twenty-four exhibition games against the best teams the Japanese could muster.

The trip was intended as a good-will tour and it was sponsored by the United States State Department and the Pepsi-Cola Company, but it was the general manager, George Weiss, who put the pressure on the boys to go. They were a pretty tired bunch of ballplayers after the grueling pennant race and the loss in the World Series, but Weiss hinted it wouldn't go well with them if they refused to make the tour. Only Phil Rizzuto, with his wife pregnant and expecting soon, could withstand the general manager's hints, thinly veiled, of punitive measures for any recalcitrant Yankee.

As it developed, with Billy Martin leading the highjinks, there wasn't a man who was sorry he went. There was even a bonus for a number of the younger ballplayers. Weiss, to sweeten the pot, allowed the boys to take their wives with them, on the house, and Johnny Kucks, Ed Robinson, and Andy Carey all took advantage of the free trip to get married a week before the Yankees set out for the Orient.

The Japanese are generally small people. Their ballplayers certainly don't have the height and weight of the American stars. But they make up for it in the intensity with which they play the game, and their fans are the most fanatical in the world.

The red-carpet treatment was out for the Yankees in every town and city they played. Hundreds of thousands of baseball-crazy Japanese lined the streets to get a look at the Yanks, as they were paraded down the avenues in royal welcome. There were two million who lined the walks to welcome the unbelieving Yankees to Tokyo. The only thing to rival these stupendous greetings had been the ticker-tape parade in downtown New York after a world championship win.

For the most part, the Yankees were dumbstruck by the baseball-crazed Japanese and just waved their hands at the fans, passing by. Casey Stengel may have been dumbstruck, too, but he had his mouth with him in the dressing room before the first exhibition game with an all-star Japanese team.

"We're on this trip, fellas," he said, "to show the Japanese how to play this game. We're going to show them what this game is all about. And something else. You fellows are going to perform 100 per cent because your jobs next year are going to depend on how you perform here. Your jobs are on the line. So you'll be hustling. You'll be winning. You'll be trying to earn a job for next year."

Stengel wanted to win every game he played, wherever he played his men. But he also knew he could get a good look at some of his new fellows, and particularly he wanted to see how well his two rookie pitchers, Johnny Kucks and Tom Sturdivant, would perform. The Japanese ballplayers weren't in a class with the Yankees, but they were good enough to test the abilities of the young hurlers. Kucks was particularly effective, as the Yanks took twenty-three games on their twenty-four-game tour, and tied one.

The Yankees played good ball, but there was more than baseball for the touring players in Japan.

There were the nightly poker games with the 180,000 yen each player got for pocket money. It was only $500 then, when the United States dollar was riding high. They wouldn't have gotten nearly that much today, with the yen soaring and the dollar doing a dip. On the trip, 10,000 yen was the minimum raise in the poker game, and the game was wild.

Then there were the parties, and particularly the wild party engineered by the hell-raising Billy Martin.

Billy and Mickey Mantle were alone at the bar of the hotel in which they were being housed in Tokyo. It was three in the morning and all the other Yankees were in their rooms, in bed and asleep. Even Whitey Ford had retired for the night.

"Let's have a party!" said Billy Martin to his pal Mickey.

"Let's have a party!" echoed Mickey.

"I'll wake 'em up!" said Billy.

And right to the phone he went, woke everyone on the team out of his sleep, including Casey Stengel.

"There's a big fight in the bar!" Billy yelled. "Mickey's getting walloped!"

And Mickey was at Billy Martin's side, banging a couple of chairs together and yelling, "Help! Help!"

Every Yankee player jumped out of his bed, every one of them, and rushed to the bar. No one was going to beat up Mickey Mantle!

They came down half dressed, in their undershorts, and some in kimonos they had bought in Tokyo. Old Casey came down in his flaming red pajamas.

At first, seeing they'd been hoaxed, they were ready to kill both Mickey and Billy Martin. But the trip had been just too much fun. There had been plenty of boozing and there was an interesting visit to an unusual geisha house. The spirit of the Yankees was too good, too high, to allow any of them to stay angry for more than a minute.

The party was on, and it went on for hours; Don Larsen, who had a great reputation for boozing, topped the party, signing Billy Martin's name and Mickey Mantle's name to everybody's bar bill.

They were high times in Japan. The boys were wearing themselves out, on the field and especially off the field.

It got so that Billy Martin suggested that maybe they ought to take it a little easy.

"Look, fellows," he said to Mickey Mantle and Whitey Ford, "it's Wednesday. How about a little sleep on Friday?"

There were a couple of other incidents on that trip, more or less amusing.

There was the visit to the Imperial Palace in Tokyo. They met Prime Minister Hatoyama, of Japan.

"Have you ever been in this area of the world before?" asked the Prime Minister, politely, making conversation.

"I've been in these parts before," said ex-Marine Hank Bauer.

"Ah yes," said the Prime Minister. "You were here before?"

"When we landed on the beach at Iwo Jima," said Hank, matter-of-fact.

For a moment there was dead silence. Iwo Jima was where the Japanese fortunes in World War II turned into a rout by American forces.

The subject was changed quickly.

Then there was the day Whitey Ford turned and hit a Japanese umpire squarely on the head with a fast ball.

The boys had been at a cocktail party before the game. There was a cocktail party before every game they played, and the boys would often enough forget about the game to be played and drink one or two or three too many.

Anyway, Whitey was pitching and the Japanese had a man on second. Ford signaled a pick-off play, but it seems like nobody caught it. No one was covering the bag when he whirled and threw the ball, except the Japanese umpire. He was hit right on his forehead.

The ball ricocheted into the outfield, where Hank Bauer, still fighting the effects of the cocktail party, just looked at the ball bouncing past him, wondering how in hell it ever got there, and the Japanese runner headed for home easily as Hank wobbled after the loose pellet.

Gil McDougald, in the meantime, had gone to see what damage the beanball had done to the Japanese umpire and just stood there in amazement as the umpire, his arms crossed, didn't move an inch.

For a moment, Gil thought the man was out cold and waited for him to fall. But the Japanese umpire just stood there as if nothing at all had happened, waiting for the game to go on.

McDougald couldn't believe it. He walked to the mound.

"Whitey," he said, "that's the tip-off on you. You hit a guy dead center from sixty feet and you don't leave a mark on him. He doesn't move a muscle. Now you know what it's like, playing the infield behind you."

He laughed. Whitey grinned. And the game went on.

It was quite a trip, that tour to Japan, but the whole Yankee squad needed a long rest after they got back home.

The State Department was pleased with the work of its emissaries. Pepsi-Cola was pleased with the advertising they got out of the Yankees. Casey came home happy, feeling that he had found himself a couple of good young pitchers. And George Weiss was relieved to know that Billy Martin hadn't created anything more than a minor incident in Japan.

As for the ballplayers, they had the time of their lives and felt well rewarded for their 1955 performance, and they went home to hunt, to fish, to travel the banquet circuit, and to get ready for the 1956 baseball season.

CHAPTER TWELVE

Billy Slows Down a Little

NOW IT WAS SPRING AGAIN, THE SPRING OF 1956, AND THE Yankees were at St. Petersburg. After the 1955 World Series, the Yankees, including Gil McDougald, had gone to Japan, and Stengel had said to him, "I want you to play shortstop on this trip."

"Wait till next spring," Gil said.

"No," Casey said, "on this trip we may need your lead."

So Gil had played shortstop in Japan. Now at St. Petersburg, Casey told reporters, "Gil said he didn't want to play shortstop. Said he didn't like it and wasn't any good at it. Maybe he's right. All I know is he plays it like he invented it. And he fits right in and makes that little toss to my manager on the field, Mr. Martin, and they make as good a double-play combination as you'll ever want to see."

Casey was looking ahead, and squarely in his sights was Phil Rizzuto, one of the authentic all-time Yankee greats. But lately he'd had good years . . . and bad years, and like Allie Reynolds, Vic Raschi, and Ed Lopat before previous seasons, Phil had said that this was his last year.

For Billy Martin, 1956 should have been one of his finest years. When Billy first came up to the Yankees he had put in two full years on the bench, soaking up Casey's knowledge, advice, and suggestions, and since 1952 Billy had been a fixture and one of the finest second basemen in baseball, and the vital cog in one of the great pennant-winning teams in baseball history. But now in spring training he could sense that he was slowing up, perhaps as much as a step. But that one step was a factor in his play, for now he was not making those smooth, effortless, fluid moves in the field, and suddenly he began to be jittery, nervous, and to lose confidence. Adding to his insecurity was the marvelous ability shown by nineteen-year-old Bobby Richardson. Billy recognized the excellence in the youngster and began to tease him.

"What are you doing here?" he demanded.

"What do you mean?" asked Richardson.

"I put something in your milk last night. Didn't you drink it?

"I wrote your draft board yesterday. You'll be hearing from them shortly."

Martin was joking, of course, but Richardson's outstanding play at second base was a real threat, and to keep ahead of him, Martin battled even harder than before, almost working himself into a frenzy.

However, more than Bobby Richardson, more than even himself, it was George Weiss who worried Billy most. He knew that Weiss had always disliked him ever since he had come up to the Yankees in 1950. He called Martin "Casey's pet" to his face and especially after the session in 1950 in which Billy had threatened to "get even."

Billy did make several tries at being friendly with the GM, but Weiss would have none of his friendship, and Billy gave up trying after a while.

Weiss, on the other hand, never let up on Billy, always looking for an excuse to get rid of him.

He called Martin into his office one day to show him a letter he had from a mother of some girl Billy had been seeing during the off-season.

"What have you got to say for yourself?" asked George Weiss.

"I didn't know it was against the rules to see a girl and take her out," said Billy.

"It's the nightclubs I'm talking about," countered Weiss. "That doesn't give the Yankees the kind of reputation we have, and want to keep."

"Now let's get this straight," shot Martin, his anger beginning to mount. "I don't see anything wrong about taking a girl to a nightclub, and certainly not when we're not playing ball. Besides, what I do with my time in winter is nobody's business but mine!"

"All right," said Weiss, frustrated for the moment and as angry as his ballplayer. "You do what you want in the winter, but I'm warning you. You watch what you do during the season."

Weiss meant to watch what Billy did during the season, too. At one time he had detectives trailing him, and a couple of his pals as well.

"Those private eyes were a joke," said Billy Martin. "One day one of them missed me going out of the hotel, so I turned back, tapped him on the shoulder, and said, 'Hey, fella, I'm leaving. Don't you want to come along?'"

George Weiss wasn't going to let up on Billy Martin, and continued to look for any reason to trade Martin and would jump down Billy's throat at the least excuse. What especially bothered Weiss was that Mickey Mantle's name was beginning to appear in the gossip columns of the New York newspapers, and for this Weiss also blamed Martin. Martin and Mantle were continuously getting into scrapes. They had missed a couple of trains and buses and a couple of times both players had been injured after wrestling bouts in the locker room. The final blow came when IRS investigators began to investigate Martin's finances. To Weiss, Billy could do no right.

But if Billy had slowed down or lost his timing at all, it wasn't very perceptible. He was still the holler kid. He continued to bat around .260, his usual pace, and he began to take over more responsibility and direct the team play from his position at second base. He became in all practicality Casey's assistant on the field and worked very well with the Yankee pitchers who suddenly found they were in trouble.

Tom Sturdivant tells of the effect Martin had on his pitching.

"I used to get so pissed off at Billy," says Tommy, "I'd get blood in my eyes.

"Sometimes I'd be out there struggling and he'd amble over

to me and say things like, 'You're just a pussy. Molly Putz could hit you. If you hit me on my nose with your fast ball, I wouldn't even feel it.'

"Boy, that next hitter knew I was throwing. I'd just wind up and give it to him.

"There was one time I had the bases loaded and I was getting tired and stiff and I didn't think I could pitch another ball, and here comes Billy, and he tells me, 'Look over there, over Yogi's shoulder,' and I look and there was this gal with her dress right up to her ass. I started to wave at her, and I look at Billy and he's laughing, and I started to laugh and relax and then I just blew the next batters right out of the game. If Billy hadn't come on, I'd have been through. With Billy's talk and assistance, I won seventeen games."

Tommy Sturdivant has a real warm spot in his heart for Billy Martin.

All in all, 1956 was a difficult year for Billy Martin. He blamed it on his Army service, which caused him to miss the 1954 season and nearly all of the 1955 season. "I found it a very tough road," he said about his return to the Yankees. "I was OK physically, and I could handle the routine plays all right. But when a play or situation called for some strategy or thinking, I had to stop for a split second to get into the game. And it wasn't till about August that I really felt good on the field." Still if Billy had slowed down or lost his confidence, it wasn't very perceptible. It was Billy's two-base hit off the Cleveland Indians' pitching great, Bob Feller, with the bases loaded, that put the Yankees in first place midway during the '56 season, a position they never relinquished as they drove on to another pennant.

CHAPTER THIRTEEN

Winning Again

THE 1956 WORLD SERIES WAS ANOTHER CLASSIC STRUGGLE between the Brooklyn Dodgers and the New York Yankees, and Billy Martin was back in World Series stride.

Billy hit one over the Ebbets Field wall for a solo home run, and Mickey Mantle hit a two-run homer off Sal (the Barber) Maglie, but Jackie Robinson got to Whitey Ford for a homer and Gil Hodges hit one for three runs. The Dodgers walked off the field with the first game of the Series.

The Dodgers took the second game as well, 13–8.

Billy hit his second home run of the Series, this time off Roger Craig, and the Yanks had their first victory in the fall classic. Then they took the next game, to even the Series.

The next game made the record books. Don Larsen, pitching without a wind-up, had the crowd roaring from the fifth inning on, as inning after inning he mowed the Dodgers down without a hit. Sal Maglie wasn't doing badly either. He didn't allow a hit till there were two down in the Yankee fourth. With two out, Mantle hit one into the right-field stands. It may have been a cheap home run, but it gave the Yankees a 1–0 lead. The lead would hold.

In the seventh inning, there was a hush in the Yankee dugout. Larsen lit up a cigarette in the runway; when he came back to the bench, he asked Martin, "Do you think I'll make it?"

Twenty-one Dodgers had come to the plate and come up empty-handed.

In the eighth, with one out, Gil Hodges smashed a hot one toward third and the Dodger fans were up on their feet, but Andy Carey caught it at his shoetops and threw to first any-

way, just in case the umpire missed the catch. Sandy Amoros
sent a soft fly to Mickey Mantle. Don Larsen had put down
twenty-four Dodgers in a row.

As the Yankees trotted into the dugout, Billy Martin called
Collins, McDougald, and Carey together.

"Nothing gets through," he said, and it might have been
that his life depended on it.

Nothing did get through.

Carl Furillo, after fouling off four pitches and as the silence
grew thicker in the ball park, lofted an easy fly to Hank Bauer.
Twenty-five Dodgers down; two to go.

Don Larsen brushed the sweat off his face and looked down
at Roy Campanella, three-time winner of the National League
Most Valuable Player award.

Campy went after the first pitch, and the Dodger fans set up
a racket as the ball headed for the stands. But the ball was foul
by yards, and the stands grew still again.

Campy drove hard into the second pitch, and this time it
was a ground ball to Billy Martin. Billy gobbled it up and
Campy was an easy out at first.

Twenty-six down and one to go. Nobody had ever pitched a
perfect World Series game—no hits, no runs, no man to reach
first.

Dale Mitchell was at the plate, pinch-hitting for Sal Maglie.
Mitchell was a lifetime .312 hitter. As a recently acquired
Dodger, he was six for fourteen as a pinch-hitter. He wasn't
particularly a long-ball hitter, but he was always a threat at the
plate. He slapped the ball through spots and he was a hard
man to strike out.

Waiting for Mitchell to get into the batter's box, Larsen
said to himself, "Please help me get through this." Maybe he
was praying.

The first pitch he threw was out of the strike zone.

"Ball one!"

The second pitch was a strike.

A fast ball missed. Two and one!

Mitchell swung at the next one and missed. Two and two.

Casey moved Mickey Mantle and Hank Bauer to the left.

Mitchell fouled the next pitch, a fast ball. The count held.

Larsen brought his hand to his chest; the hesitation and then a low, outside fast ball.

Babe Pinelli jerked up his right thumb.

Strike three!

The game was over and Don Larsen had made history.

Yogi Berra was all over him. Larsen had to carry the exuberant catcher all the way to the dugout, as the fans screamed their appreciation of the historic pitching performance, the first no-hit, no-run victory in a World Series.

Bob Turley pitched his heart out in the sixth game of the Series. The game was 0–0 at the end of the regulation nine innings. In the last half of the tenth, with Junior Gilliam on second and Duke Snider on first, Jackie Robinson lined one deep toward left field. Enos Slaughter was playing shallow so that a bloop single couldn't score the winning run. As the ball left Robinson's bat, he took a step forward. It was a mistake. The ball sailed over his head and Gilliam scored the winning run to even the Series.

Turley, understandably, felt pretty rotten about the defeat. He had pitched the best game of his career and lost.

Casey Stengel felt just about as bad as his young pitcher, for the pitcher.

Billy Martin was fuming. "Goddamn!"

He moved up front in the bus taking the team back from Ebbets Field. He sat himself down next to Casey.

"If you're going to keep playing that fucking National League bobo out there," he spat (the National League bobo being Enos Slaughter, purchased from the St. Louis Cardinals), "we're going to blow the Series!"

"You think he should have made that catch?" asked Casey.

"You're damned right he should have made it!" came back Billy Martin.

"Who would you play?" asked old Case.

"You'd better put Elston out there," said Billy. Elston was

Elston Howard. "And you'd better get Skowron's ass back to first base!"

And that's the way the Yankees lined up for the seventh and deciding game of the 1956 World Series, Elston Howard in left field and Moose Skowron at first.

Howard hit a home run in the fourth inning and the Moose hit a grand-slam homer in the seventh to bring home the game, 9–0, and one more world championship for Casey and the New York club.

Old Case looked for Billy in the clubhouse after the game, found him in the middle of the wild celebration, and said, "You're a smart little bastard, aren't you!"

They hugged each other, the two men who loved each other, the father figure and teacher Casey Stengel, and the son figure, who showed he knew a thing or two about managing a ball club, Billy Martin.

There was good feeling and no little joy they shared together that afternoon. In less than a year, Billy Martin would cut Casey Stengel dead.

CHAPTER FOURTEEN

Weiss Trades Billy

GEORGE WEISS, WHOSE ONE PURPOSE IN LIFE SEEMED TO BE TO get rid of Billy Martin, put it on the line for Billy at spring training in '57.

"Get into trouble just one more time," he warned him, "and that will be all!"

Midway into May, George Weiss got his big chance, and he jumped at it.

Mickey Mantle and Whitey Ford arranged a party for Billy Martin's twenty-ninth birthday. His birthday was on the sixteenth of May, but the party was scheduled for the fifteenth. The sixteenth was an open day in the baseball schedule and they figured there'd be an entire day to sleep off the celebration they had planned.

There was dinner at Danny's Hideaway, a popular New York restaurant at the time. Mickey Mantle, Whitey Ford, Hank Bauer, Yogi Berra, Johnny Kucks, and their wives, and Martin, without a date, were the celebrants.

After dinner, it was to the Waldorf-Astoria Hotel to hear the great songs of "crying" Johnny Ray, and then on to the posh Copacabana nightclub to take in a performance by the great Sammy Davis, Jr.

Their wives with them, the boys were on their best behavior, and Billy was decorous and gallant, as he always was in the presence of the wives of his teammates. It was a comparatively quiet and thoroughly enjoyable evening, until some fat drunk, sitting at the table next to them, began to abuse Sammy Davis.

"Hey! You jungle bunny!" yelled the drunk, and Sammy Davis, singing and dancing, stopped the music to walk to the front of the stage.

"I want to thank you very much for that remark," he said to the drunk. "I'll remember it."

Sammy began to sing and dance again, but the drunk wouldn't let up on him.

"Why in hell don't you shut up?" Hank Bauer yelled at the souse.

"Why don't you try and make me shut up?" said the drunk pugnaciously.

There were a few other people at that other table. They were all bowlers and were apparently at the Copa to do their own celebrating.

"Yeah," they needled, "why don't you make him shut up?"

For half an hour the threats and challenges bounced from party to party.

Billy Martin, finally fed up, his celebration ruined, said, "We're here to have a good time. You've been sprouting all night. If you want to talk about this somewhere else, we can settle it outside and let the other people here enjoy themselves."

"Let's go," said the fat drunk.

Hank Bauer and the fat man were up on their feet and headed for the nearest door, which led to the men's room. Billy and Mickey were right behind him.

One of the other bowlers, who turned out to be the fat drunk's brother, stopped Billy.

"Keep Bauer away from him and we'll keep my brother quiet," promised the bowler.

By the time Mickey and Billy could get to the men's room, however, the fat drunk was out cold on the floor.

"I never touched the man," said Hank.

A number of the other bowlers were in the men's room, as well as a couple of Copacabana bouncers.

It was one of the bouncers who took care of the fat man, probably for interrupting the Copa show, if not to pay him back for his racial slurs.

At least that's what Hank Bauer thought, and Billy, Mickey, and the rest of the birthday celebrants were inclined to agree with him.

The Yankees left the Copa as fast as they could, and through a kitchen exit.

At four-thirty that morning, a reporter for the New York *Daily News* called Hank Bauer at home to tell him a man had sworn out a warrant for his arrest on assault and battery.

The *Daily News* ran a banner headline on its front page: HANK BAUER IN BRAWL AT COPA.

George Weiss read the headline and almost had a stroke. He had his assistant, Roy Hamey, call Bauer, Billy Martin, and Whitey Ford, telling them to get down to the Yankee Fifth Avenue office in half an hour. If they weren't in the office in a half hour, they'd be fined a thousand dollars each.

"No way I can get from Lake Success to the office in thirty minutes," said Ford.

But it was no time before Weiss had every man who had been at the Copa that night in his office.

"Nobody did nothing to nobody," said Yogi Berra.

The story he got from the rest of the men was identical. The fat man was knocked out in the men's room before Hank Bauer could reach him.

George Weiss wasn't satisfied. He was sure Billy Martin was at the bottom of the whole fracas. It was his golden opportunity to ditch Billy at last.

Dan Topping, co-owner of the Yankees, backed up Weiss. He slapped a one-thousand-dollar fine on Martin, Mantle, Berra, Ford, and Bauer. He was generous to the younger Johnny Kucks, and fined him only five hundred dollars.

Gil McDougald, who hadn't been to the party at the Copa, blew his top.

"You go down to the commissioner's office and demand that they rescind that fine," he yelled at his roommate, Hank Bauer. "Nobody is going to tell us when and where I can take my wife out for dinner and a night on the town."

The fines had been levied before the accused Yankees presented themselves before a grand jury. Topping was acting like a judge and jury all in one.

When the players did get to that grand jury in the State

Criminal Courts Building in lower Manhattan, the district attorney, promptly dismissed the case for insufficient evidence.

Casey Stengel's comment on the whole affair, later, was, "The reason they had the party in the Copa was that they didn't want to hold it in a hospital."

Casey joked about the whole business but, with the June 15 trading deadline just a month away, he was worried; he was worried for Billy Martin. He knew that Weiss held all the cards now in the Weiss-Martin feud.

Billy was worried, too, though deep down in his heart he couldn't even imagine being traded away from Casey and the Yankees.

Early in June, the hot-tempered Martin got himself into another brawl, this time on the diamond, feeding Weiss a little more ammunition in his battle to get rid of Billy.

The Yankees were playing the Chicago White Sox and there was bad blood between them.

Art Ditmar knocked down Larry Doby with a pitch that came near beaning him. The day before, Al Cicotte, pitching for the Yanks, had nearly beaned Minnie Minoso, and Minnie hurled his bat out to the mound on the next pitch, nearly taking Cicotte's legs from under him.

Doby hit the dirt on the Ditmar pitch and the ball rolled to the backstop, Ditmar coming to the plate to defend against a possible score by the runner on second.

Doby, getting the dust off his uniform, said quietly but intensely, "Do that again, Ditmar, and I'll slip a knife into your back."

"Go fuck yourself," said Ditmar, and Doby swung at him.

Both benches were out on the field, fast.

Bill Skowron wrestled Doby to the ground. Walt Dropo went at Skowron to get him off Doby. Enos Slaughter began to tangle with Dropo. Whitey Ford was out there, too, and, of course, Billy Martin. Even Casey was up and at them, jawing away at White Sox outfielder Jim Rivera.

Skowron's uniform was ripped to shreds. Slaughter's shirt was all torn.

The umpires threw Doby, Dropo, and Slaughter out of the game. Ditmar, for some reason that was never explained, was allowed to remain in the game.

"What did Doby say to you?" Billy asked the Yankee pitcher.

"He said he was going to stick me with a knife," Ditmar said.

And without another word, Martin rushed at Doby and began swinging.

It was Billy Martin's last fight as a Yankee ballplayer. Two days later, before June 15, midnight, the trading deadline, he was informed that he had been traded to the Kansas City Athletics.

"Well, you're gone," said Casey.

It was a bad moment for both of them. The tears welled up in Billy Martin's eyes. He was overcome—he couldn't talk.

"You were the smartest little player I ever had," said Casey.

Billy couldn't speak.

"You got me the hit when I needed it," continued the old man. "You did everything I asked you to do."

Billy still said nothing. He turned his back on the man he had loved so much and walked out into the locker room.

Mickey Mantle and Whitey Ford were crying.

"He's the best friend I ever had," said Mickey. "It's like losing a brother."

The Yanks had traded Martin to the A's for Harry (Suitcase) Simpson, a thirty-one-year-old outfielder, and pitcher Ryne Duren.

"For Simpson?" asked Enos Slaughter, who couldn't believe it, and Slaughter was never overfond of Billy Martin. "Somebody must be crazy."

It was six years after that eventful afternoon before Billy Martin would speak to Casey again. Billy would write an article for a sports magazine telling how much he loved the man, and how much he had learned from old Case but, much as the old man tried to break the silence of his "fresh kid," Billy would never answer a "hello" or a shout across the diamond by a regretful Stengel.

Billy explained, "My heart was broken because I felt that a father, not just a manager, had let me down."

When finally years later at a baseball meeting in Houston, Martin bumped into Casey in the lobby of a hotel, and said, simply, "Hi, Casey," the old man just jumped out of his chair and began to talk to his "little bastard" as if they had never been separated, not even for a day.

"It's been a long time since drinks," said the governor of North Carolina to the governor of South Carolina.

It had been a long time since the "son" and the "father" had gotten together, and all those years between had not been good ones for Billy Martin.

CHAPTER FIFTEEN

Six Trades in Six Years

"ANYBODY WHO SAYS HE LIKES TO BE TRADED IS A LIAR," SAID
Billy Martin.

From 1957 to 1961, he was traded six times.

"I've been bouncing around like a ball," he said.

When Billy was traded to the Kansas City Athletics, he
went from a pennant winner to a perennial tail-ender. No one
could have felt good about that kind of trade. Martin went to
the Athletics a bitter young man. He knew that George Weiss
had engineered the deal purely because of a personal feud. He
felt that Casey Stengel could have put up a fight against the
trade, and didn't. Casey, Martin believed, in the clutch, had
failed in a test of loyalty. Loyalty was a keystone in Billy Martin's concept of a code of honor.

Still, he played his best for the Athletics, in what was a
losing cause, it soon became apparent to him. He gave it the
old try, whooping and hollering it up, trying to spark the club,
the way he had inspired the Yankees; it just didn't work with
the Kansas City team; they were a losing ball club; nothing,
not even Billy Martin's drive, was going to change the
indifferent attitude on the club.

"He did everything we asked him to do," said Parke Carroll,
general manager of the Kansas City team, echoing Casey Stengel's critique of Martin.

"I'll bust my tail off for them," Billy said, putting on a Kansas City uniform for the first time, and in his first game for the
club, and against his old teammates, the New York Yankees,
he smashed a single in the fourth inning and a go-ahead home
run in the eighth.

It was strange for Billy, playing against the Yanks, stranger getting cheered for his efforts at beating them. He had never worn anything but a Yankee uniform in the big leagues, and, at heart, he would remain a Yankee all his baseball years.

"What am I trying to do?" he would ask himself.

Nothing he tried to do seemed to work with the Kansas City A's.

"After a while," said Billy Martin, "I began to say to myself, 'What's the use?' and 'Why don't I mind my own business?'"

He was a happier man when at the end of the season he was traded to the Detroit Tigers.

"Sure we traded him," said Parke Carroll to the press, "but we got a lot of help for our team. We got a catcher, a good pitcher, and a good outfielder. There were six clubs bidding for Billy Martin. We took the best deal we were offered."

The Kansas City Athletics got catcher Frank House, pitcher Duke Maas, and outfielder Bill Tuttle. The Tigers got the man they believed would win them the American League pennant.

"Now that we've got Billy Martin," said Jack Tighe, the Tigers' manager, "we've got better than a good shot at the flag. Billy's the kind of guy we needed, a natural leader. He knows how to win and he'll show the rest of the club how to win."

And Billy was as pleased as Tighe with the deal, glad to be freed from a losing ball club, happy to be with a team that would make a race for the pennant.

"A fellow who has been with the Yankees," Billy said, "can't be happy playing on a losing club. Don't get me wrong. I'm not knocking Kansas City. The Tigers are contenders and I'll give them my best shot."

And then with a smile, "Playing in Kansas City is better than working."

But things didn't turn out too well for Billy Martin in Detroit, either.

Tighe made a mistake, not entirely his own, playing Martin at shortstop. Martin told him he could play anywhere in the infield.

There is more pressure on the shortstop than there is on the player at second. The shortstop covers more ground, has to

have a stronger arm than the second baseman. And he has to
be steady and sure of himself.

"Billy is too high-strung for that position," said Gil McDougald; and he was right.

The shortstop is more vulnerable to making errors than the
second baseman, and Billy Martin was no exception to the
statistics. And the more errors he made playing short, the more
tense he became. It showed up in his batting, too.

Still a Yankee at heart, Billy inaugurated songfests on the
bus trips and brought along song sheets when he discovered
the boys didn't know the words to the songs. It just didn't
work.

The Tigers had a bad year, finished in fifth place, and in
1959 Billy was traded to the Cleveland Indians.

Frank Lane paid a price for Martin. Billy was still the
battling, fighting asset the clubs around the league wanted for
their organization, with the single exception of George Weiss
and Company. Lane gave up Ray Narleski and Don Mossi,
who had been the two best relief pitchers in baseball for five
years, to get Martin the sparkplug he figured would drive the
Indians on to the pennant.

John McHale, the Tigers' GM said, "We weren't anxious to
give up Billy Martin. Washington and Boston both wanted
him badly. We just couldn't pass up Mossi and Narleski when
Cleveland offered us in a trade for him."

Billy Martin said, "The trouble with them is too much pub-
licity, too much money, not enough spirit. I could get Hank
Bauer, Gene Woodling, Mickey Mantle, maybe the whole
Yankee team up. I couldn't do anything in Detroit."

The Tigers, in fact, resented Billy's gung-ho style of playing
the game. They didn't respond to his hollering, jockeying, needling.

"You win a few, you lose a few."

That wasn't the way Billy Martin saw it.

It was another disappointing year for Billy, who had started
the '58 season with such high hopes. Playing for the Tigers
made him miss playing for the Yankees more than ever.

"You can't lead a club," he said, "if it doesn't want to be lead."

Cleveland didn't prove to be good for Billy Martin either, though he went back to playing second base, where he was more comfortable. He put the blame for a rather poor showing directly on the head of the Indians' manager, Joe Gordon.

"We had a winner for sure," said Billy Martin, "but Gordon blew it."

"I seldom talked to him," said Billy, "because he didn't talk too much to me. What I do know," continued Billy, "is that he talks a lot about me. Every time I pick up a paper in Cleveland I read Gordon said I can't make the double play, or I can't do this and I can't do that."

Gretchen Winkler, an ex-airline stewardess out of Nebraska, the girl Billy Martin would marry at the end of the season in Cleveland, went to the record books and furnished Billy with a bit of information he might have used as ammunition against his manager. She discovered that Gordon, when he had been a second baseman, made 258 errors in the field in 12 years; Billy Martin had made only 79 in his 10 years at second base.

"I can't be too bad," said Billy, later.

Billy's jaw was fractured by a pitched ball in the middle of the season. Thrown by Tex Clevenger, the pitch hit Billy high on the cheekbone and fractured seven face bones. His eye was damaged as a result of the pitch and he was fed intravenously for several days. The injury kept him out of the lineup a good part of the year, and when he finally did return he never again was his old confident self at the plate.

But even when Billy's jaw mended, Gordon didn't put him back into the lineup. Billy wound up the year playing in less than half the club's schedule with a batting average of .260 and only 24 runs batted in.

"Gordon just didn't like me," said Billy Martin. "Something personal, I guess, and he never told me, but it cost him the pennant. He took me out of the game when we were moving and put me back when we were in a slump. His personal feelings didn't hurt me; they hurt the club."

Next stop, Cincinnati, out of the American League and for the first time a National Leaguer. And Billy Martin was only one of the three players Cleveland gave Cincinnati for their star second baseman, Johnny Temple. Billy Martin's fortune had sunk pretty low; there wasn't a club in the American League that had put in a bid for the onetime sparkplug of the champion New York Yankees.

Cincinnati proved a disaster, too, in more ways than one.

"I'm not looking for any fights," he said, moving over to the Redlegs. "The doc just told me I'm going to have a glass jaw the next five months."

But Billy couldn't hold out for five months, and it cost him more than $22,500.

The Reds were playing the Chicago Cubs, and Jim Brewer, a rookie pitcher with the Cubs, brushed Billy back with a hard fast one. It was aimed right at Billy's head.

Billy's reaction was immediate and as always tempestuous. He hurled his bat at the pitcher, the bat missed, and Billy walked out to the mound to pick up the bat and to say a few choice words to the rookie hurler.

Brewer, a good three inches taller and twenty pounds heavier than Martin, delivered a few choice street words and a bit of advice on his own to the Reds' second baseman.

Their disagreement didn't last too long before a furious Martin slammed a tremendous right to Brewer's jaw. The punch busted Brewer's face to a pulp.

Immediately, the combatants were joined by their teammates, and when the melee was finally broken up, Brewer had to be taken to the hospital, where he underwent two operations for a broken orbital bone above the eye.

Jim Brewer was out for the season.

Billy Martin insisted that he had nothing to do with the breaking of that orbital bone, that some other player may have done it.

"I hit him on the chin," said Billy.

Nor would Billy forgive Brewer his beanball, for all the trou-

ble the pitcher was suffering. He was sorry Brewer had been so
badly hurt, but he was never sorry for the punch.

"It's all right if they brush you back," said Billy Martin. "A
pitcher has to do that every once in a while to loosen up the
batter. And it's all right if they hit you on your shoulder, in
your back, your leg, your stomach. But when you throw at a
batter's head, or over his head, you move into the ball instinctively; and that's murder!"

The National League office didn't see it quite the way Billy
saw it. They fined him $500 for the incident, and suspended
him for five days.

Later, the Chicago Cubs and Jim Brewer sued Billy for more
than $1 million, and Billy finally had to pay up $22,500 in settlement of the suit.

The entire bill for that one punch was $23,000. It was a
mighty expensive punch Billy Martin threw at Jim Brewer, and
it didn't help Billy's stay with the Cincinnati Redlegs. He was
traded in 1961 to the Milwaukee Braves. This time there were
no players and there was comparatively little cash involved in
the transaction.

"When a fellow bounces around the way I've been bounced
around the last few years, people get the idea that you must be
all washed up. Well, I know I'm not washed up. I know, too,
the only way I can prove it is on the field."

Evidently Billy didn't prove it to the satisfaction of Milwaukee.

Billy wanted to show his stuff on that team in the worst
way. The Braves had finished at the top and no lower than second for six years' running. It was a winner, like his old Yankees.

But Milwaukee picked up Frank Bolling to play second, before the season got under way, and Billy was on the bench. He
was in only six games for the Braves, each time as a pinch-hitter, and was then traded, on the first of June, to the Minnesota
Twins. This time a minor-league player and a little cash were
all that the Twins paid for the once highly desired Billy Martin.

Billy played regularly at second base for the Minnesota club, but he turned in the lowest batting average of his career, .246, and committed 17 errors. The sparkplug, it seemed, had lost its reflexes.

In the spring of 1962, Billy Martin was released by the Minnesota Twins while the club was still in spring training, ending an incredible eleven-year major-league career. Martin's career as a ballplayer had come to an end. His reputation and morale were at the lowest points in his life.

"I had been knocked around so badly," he said. "The things they said about me. And when I was released, I was determined to come back. I thought I had to eat humble pie. I had to stay in the game and prove to people in baseball that I was a different person. I'd let them know the real Billy Martin."

CHAPTER SIXTEEN

Coaching the Twins

CALVIN GRIFFITH, LIKE CASEY STENGEL, HAD DEVELOPED A PAternal attitude toward Billy Martin and, like only Casey Stengel before him, saw the managerial possibilities in the ballplayer.

When Billy was released as an active player in the spring of 1962 by the Minnesota Twins he was offered one hundred thousand dollars to play ball in Japan. He turned that offer down. He still felt he could make the difference between a winning and losing ball club, and his pride wouldn't let him quit the American baseball scene.

It was then that Calvin Griffith, owner of the Twins, suggested that Billy stay on with his organization.

"We'd like you with us, Billy," he said.

Billy had thought about managing after he was through as a ballplayer, and then had forgotten about it. He didn't think the "troublemaker" tag George Weiss pinned on him would do him any good with the front offices around the leagues. He didn't think the label, "the Graziano of baseball" would help him either.

Still, he thought, and said, that if he didn't get the chance to manage a team, somebody would be making a mistake.

"I could do a good job," he said. "I could lead a team and spark them as a player. Why couldn't I lead them as a manager? I know how to handle men, and that's the secret of managing."

Billy could go on for hours about his potential as a manager, and he wasn't modest about his potential, either.

"It's not only the fundamentals of the game that I know," he said. "I know how to execute. I could teach the younger players and they would respect my knowledge. I've got enough background and experience with championship teams, and the players will know that I can help them at every position on the field. I know I can do a hell of a job if I ever get the chance to manage."

And time would prove that Billy Martin knew what he was talking about, but managing was far from Calvin Griffith's mind when he spoke to Billy Martin back in 1962.

The job he offered Billy with the Twins was as a "troubleshooter" and scout at ten thousand dollars a year.

"You can be with us for a long time," said Griffith, by way of inducement.

Billy Martin talked the proposition over with his wife, Gretchen.

"She is a levelheaded woman," said Billy, "and intelligent. And a very pretty woman," he added, "and I couldn't have picked a better girl."

It was time for some stability in his life. He had been living as a nomad baseball player for some eleven years.

In addition, their son was growing up, Billy Joe needed him, and there was the house they wanted to buy in suburban Richfield, near the Twins' baseball park. He needed a steady job for a while at least.

Billy took the job. For three years he worked as a scout for the Minnesota club; then Griffith, making good on his promise, brought Billy back to the action on the diamond, as third-base coach for the Twins.

Even before spring training, Griffith suggested that Billy devote some time with the moody shortstop of the Minnesota Twins, Zoilo Versalles. Billy began to work with Versalles in February. He was that eager to put on a baseball uniform once again and to be part of the action.

Billy had learned from Casey that you treat certain players with kid gloves, others you scream and blister out. He used both approaches with Versalles. He coaxed him and blasted him to his face, but he was always sure to be alone with the temperamental shortstop when he gave him hell. Versalles couldn't take a dressing down in front of anybody else, particularly in front of anybody playing ball with him.

And Billy worked wonders with the young ballplayer. He got him to be more aggressive when he was up at the plate. He got him to use his natural speed on the basepaths. He taught Zoilo how to release the ball more quickly, throwing to first base and the short, snap throw to second base for the double play. At the end of the 1965 season, Versalles improved his all-around play so much that he won the American League's Most Valuable Player award. Billy also devoted time to Cesar Tovar, another infielder who developed into a fine player.

In 1965, with manager Sam Mele directing the team and Billy coaching, the Twins went from a sixth-place finish in 1964 to first place and the pennant in 1965. Billy once again had recaptured the initial spark that he had as a Yankee and ignited the Twins with his winning spirit. He was the bounciest and noisiest Twin on the field. He was out on the field with his glove during the practice session. He was out there on the field, working with the infield, practicing, laughing, joking, driving the players on, working with individual players. He was the Kid, with his old No. 1 on his shirt. He was always Billy the Kid, and his drive, his needling, his bustle, and his sound baseball fundamentals produced results.

He drew lines all over the infield. One of the lines was to indicate where a base runner should start to make his turn in rounding the bases. There was also a line twenty feet to the right of second, another forty feet from the bag.

"Inside the first line," instructed Billy Martin, "the second baseman tosses the ball underhand to second base, covered by the shortstop, to make a force play. Between the two lines, the second baseman throws hard, side arm. Beyond the second line, he has to pivot to make the throw."

The Twins never had a coach who drilled them and taught the fundamentals and strategy as coach Billy Martin; and they ate it up.

Sam Mele, manager of the Twins, was euphoric, welcoming Billy back to the coaching staff in 1966. The other coaches on the club—Jim Lemon, Hal Naragon, and especially Johnny Sain—were somewhat less enthusiastic. They didn't like his gung-ho mannerisms. They didn't care particularly for the way he socialized with the players, as if he were still one of the boys. And they certainly didn't like the way he'd take charge on the field. Johnny Sain, who had done so much for the Minnesota Twins' pitchers, was actually ready to give up his job because of his disdain for Billy Martin.

Spring training went well enough, although Billy and the Twins' traveling secretary, Howard Fox, had a few harsh words between them every now and then. Howard Fox was a mild-mannered man, a sort of southern gentleman type; Billy's brashness rubbed him the wrong way, and Martin wasn't much impressed by Fox's genteel manners. Nevertheless, they managed a surface peace between them, and Billy concentrated his efforts on the ballplayers, getting them into shape for the 1966 pennant race.

"We've got to get off to a good start," he urged, "we've got to get off quickly, win some games, that'll give the players confidence, and once they have that confidence, we're gonna be a tough team to beat.

"Look at the schedule," he said. "It's all in our favor. We play second-division teams early. And in September we play all of the contenders. It will be much tougher than last year. We have got to get the players off to a fast start, 'cause in September it will be a toss-up.

Billy Martin was making sense looking far ahead into September.

"Martin can be best described as a tightly wound box of noise. Wherever he goes, you hear a racket," wrote a Minnesota sportswriter. "You don't look for Martin. You listen for him."

Sometimes people listened too closely, and sometimes Billy said too much, and not always in language suitable for the ears of young ladies. In any case, Howard Fox and Billy Martin got into a squabble about the use of language on a plane from Minneapolis to Washington early in July of 1966.

The Yankees were on that plane, too, on the way to New York, and all was well until some of the Yankees got into a row with a steward who had a bad habit of snatching drinks out of the hands of passengers.

At one point, the steward took a drink out of the hand of Roger Maris and ordered the stewardess on board to cut off further service.

Clete Boyer and Hal Reniff had a few choice remarks for the steward, remarks they would never make to a stewardess.

"Quiet down," said Ralph Houk, the Yankee manager.

Howard Fox asked Martin to see whether he couldn't quiet down his old Yankee buddies.

"None of my business!" said Billy.

Billy didn't like being asked, and Fox didn't much like Billy's response to his request. They kept at each other till they got to Washington. On the bus from Dulles International Airport, the situation became angry. It boiled over when they got to the hotel lobby.

Fox handed out the room keys to the team.

Fox said he threw Billy's keys down on the front of the desk.

Billy said Fox threw the keys into his face.

"You did that on purpose!" yelled Billy. "Someday I'm going to take you outside and beat the living hell out of you!"

Fox, who wears glasses, took them off.

"How about now? Right here?" he challenged.

Billy Martin moved in fast, and Fox was on his knees from several hard punches.

Sometime after the fight they shook hands, but Billy had something to worry about. Fox had been a close friend of the Twins' president, Calvin Griffith, for some twenty years.

"Somebody told Martin it would be him or me with the club. I never said anything like that to Calvin. I don't want anything like that to happen."

Howard Fox remained the gentleman, but he never forgave Billy Martin for the incident.

Billy was fined $100 by Calvin Griffith for "using mild invectives" on that trip to Washington from Dulles International on the Minnesota chartered bus while ladies were present.

Joe Duffy at Duffy's Bar in Minneapolis had the boys at the bar chip in $1.00 each to pay that fine. In four minutes he collected $130, but, said Duffy, "I'm thinking of making it $200 just in case Billy Martin gets into trouble again."

Billy had his fans in Minnesota.

He had his fans all over the country.

As early as May 1, 1966, there were stories in the sports pages—in New York, in Kansas City, in Chicago, all over the place—that Billy Martin was scheduled to manage the Tigers, the Twins, the Yankees in 1967. And, of course, there were the usual denials for the press.

"There's not a bit of truth in it," said Jim Campbell, general manager of the Detroit Tigers.

"Jim assured me he is not tampering with any of my men," said Calvin Griffith.

"Nobody has approached me," said Billy Martin. "It's very flattering, but this is the first I've heard about it. Another thing, I'm not rushing into a job as manager of a weak organization. When I make a move it will be with a first-rate club. Anyway, I'm happy here as a coach for the Twins. I've got a new home, my wife and boy are with me, and I want to stay here."

Billy Martin was still coaching at third base for the Minnesota Twins at the end of '66, and again at the beginning of '67, but the rumors continued and became more persistent. Charles Finley, owner of the Kansas City Athletics, seemed particularly eager to hire Billy Martin as a manager for 1968. On October 12, 1967, he asked Calvin Griffith for Billy's phone number, and Griffith gave it to him.

Sam Mele had recommended Martin to Finley, and Griffith said, "I wouldn't stand in Billy's way to manager."

But Billy Martin did not take the job with the Charles Finley club. Maybe Billy figured out what it would be like working for him before a lot of others did.

Billy stayed on with Calvin Griffith and the Twins through the 1967 season, and when he did move, it was a move that was suggested by Cal Griffith. It was one of the more important decisions in the life of Billy Martin, for that move was to change his life.

CHAPTER SEVENTEEN

Manager of the Twins

THE DENVER BEARS, A MINNESOTA FARM CLUB, WAS IN SEVENTH place, and going nowhere in 1968. A delegation from the Bears' front office came to ask Calvin Griffith, the Twins' president, for some help. Specifically, they asked that the manager of the Triple-A Denver team be fired, and for Billy Martin to replace him.

Griffith's first reaction was a flat "No!"

Then he said, "I don't think Martin would be interested in the job."

But there were a number of men who thought it would be a good thing for the Twins to send Billy over to the Bears. Actually, this was the anti-Martin sector of the Twins' front office. It was their chance to get Billy out of their hair. And more, they were pretty sure that the Kid would mess up the job in Denver and they'd be able to get rid of Martin for good, and out of the Twins' organization.

Griffith offered Billy the job, and an increase in salary.

Billy liked his coaching job with the Twins. He had achieved the kind of security that every child of the Great Depression spends his life seeking.

"Still, I realize that if I'm ever going to manage in the major leagues, I've got to have some experience as a manager. It's a necessity."

Billy was surprised, uncertain, and he was unsure. He had his doubts about moving out of a safe, secure job as coach.

"I didn't want to go," he said. "I was happy for once in my life. I liked where I lived, my friends. I had a beautiful home, a comfortable, safe lifestyle. Why give it up?"

He brought his dilemma home to his wife, Gretchen. They

talked about it all night. And Gretchen urged him to make the change.

"I knew he wouldn't be happy if he didn't try," she said. "I told him he had to go to Denver to prove he could manage."

"I couldn't sleep all night," said Billy.

"There'll always be a place for you in the Minnesota organization," said Calvin Griffith.

Billy took the job.

"I'll tell you," said one of the Minnesota players, "Denver won't finish last. They wouldn't dare."

Billy took over a disorganized, demoralized Denver team.

The Bears had won only eight games, while losing twenty-two, when Billy Martin arrived on the scene. The first thing he did was to call a team meeting to inspire a semblance of discipline.

"Everyone wears a shirt, a tie, and a jacket in public," he ordered. "You can wear your hair and your sideburns long, but keep them neat. It's a little thing, but pride starts with little things. I want us to look like gentlemen, not hippies. I want you to eat, drink, sleep baseball twenty-four hours a day. I want each one of you to take pride in winning. Winning is the only thing that counts."

It sounded like a speech he had heard Casey Stengel deliver in the clubhouse.

Billy didn't win the league pennant in 1968. Except for the potentially great Graig Nettles, he had an ordinary group of players to work with. They won 65 of the 115 games they played under Martin, a complete turnaround that had the entire league and the Denver fans excited. He had proven to himself that he could take a losing ball club and that he could provide the impetus to win. He had faced a challenge and won.

Now rumors about Billy's move into the big leagues as a manager began to surface again. Calvin Griffith took a couple of trips to watch his Denver team play under the Kid, and he was impressed.

The Twins, who had dropped from first place to seventh in 1968, fired manager Cal Ermer, who had replaced Sam Mele.

It soon became an open secret that Billy was headed for the manager's job in Minnesota.

In October of 1968, Calvin Griffith made the secret public property. He named Billy "the Kid" Martin the Twins' manager for 1969.

"You people in the news media," said Griffith, "certainly helped me make a decision. I've never seen such a campaign in my life. I feel that Billy has the ability to be another Casey Stengel."

Martin, an emotional tinge in his voice, called the appointment "a dream, a challenge . . . the kind of challenge I've always loved, and one which I'm sure will bring out the best in me and the Minneapolis ball club."

Privately, Griffith was worried. He knew he would have trouble getting Billy to follow directives from the front office.

"I know," said Griffith, "that I'll be sitting on a keg of dynamite."

Seventy-eight-year-old Casey Stengel, in a telephone conversation, had no doubts about Billy at all.

"The Kid has confidence," he said. "He always had that. He thinks there is a way of winning every ball game and he thinks he knows how to do it. The players will want to play for him. He'll get the most out of them. He was the greatest at psychology and how to inject it. He was an aggressive ballplayer. He'll be an aggressive manager."

There was much love in what Casey had to say about the Kid, and much horse sense, too.

John Roseboro, the catcher for the Minnesota Twins, spoke for most of the club's ballplayers, and soberly, as well.

"If Martin can run the club the way he wants to run it," he said, "and have the authority he should have, he'll make one helluva manager."

Billy quickly established his style of managing a ball club with a style of aggressive play that quickly infused the Twins with a new and daring spirit. The Twins had always been a hard-hitting club; they had some of the American League's greatest hitters—Rod Carew, Tony Oliva, Harmon Killebrew,

John Roseboro, Graig Nettles. But Billy wanted them to run the bases too, something they had not previously done. He worked with Rod Carew and Tony Oliva and showed them how to wait on the ball and how to hit to the opposite field behind a base runner; he taught them to watch the opposing pitcher closely for any slight hint of the pitch to come, and he showed them how to steal signs from the opposing coaches.

Stealing home became a specialty with Martin's Twins.

"I've always said home is the easiest base to steal," said Billy Martin, "if you watch the pitcher and time it right."

By mid-July, Carew had stolen home six times in six attempts.

Opposing hurlers stopped taking the full wind-up with a Twin on third.

Martin took Carew aside and worked patiently on his swing. He urged Carew to cut down on his swing, to become a line-drive hitter, to spray his hits to all fields, and Carew went on to lead the Twins and within a year became the American League's batting champion with a .332 average—an increase of 40 points above his 1967 batting average.

The Twins got off poorly once the season started, losing their first four games, but a blistering tongue lashing from manager Martin fired the explosive Twins and they ran up seven consecutive wins to take over first place.

The heads-up baseball, daring base running, and tremendous home-run slugging by Harmon Killebrew plus effective pitching by Jim Kaat, Dave Boswell, and Ron Perranoski kept the Twins out in front the rest of the season.

All was well with the Kid, the team, and with Calvin Griffith, too, at the beginning of the season. But that was it. In mid-May, Billy Martin exploded at the manner in which the front office was shifting his players around and demoting them to the farm clubs. He didn't like the operation of the farm clubs and he said as much, attacking both Sherry Robertson, who was responsible for the farm system, and his assistant, George Brophy.

Unfortunately, Sherry Robertson carried a little more weight

with Calvin Griffith than did Billy Martin. Sherry Robertson
was Griffith's brother-in-law.

Billy was called into the office. It was three against one. And
Billy had to take it. The meeting with the brass wound up
with the Kid making his apologies to Griffith's brother-in-law
and George Brophy.

But Billy knew he was right, and he hated himself for the
way he accepted the dictum of Calvin Griffith and made his
apologies. Farm teams are supposed to develop players and
send them on to the parent club; else they have no purpose at
all.

"If Brophy wasn't wearing glasses," said Billy, still seething,
"I would have sailed into him."

It was for the best, at the moment, anyway, that the Kid
had restrained himself; but there were two more men in the
Minnesota anti-Martin contingent.

There was a more dramatic and more damaging incident for
Billy Martin some few months later, in August.

Dave Boswell, the Twins' pitcher, had been ordered to run
twenty laps to keep in good physical shape for his chores on
the mound. Billy required all his pitchers to run a certain number of laps.

But Boswell, the team flake and a temperamental man, ran
only two laps and then cut off the field.

Art Fowler, Billy's pitching coach, dutifully reported this
lapse in discipline to his boss, and Billy had a few hard words
to say to his pitcher the next day.

Boswell didn't take the dressing down too well.

"I'll get Fowler for this," he threatened. "The squealer!"

"Fowler is working for me," said Billy. "It's his job to report
to me."

That didn't change Boswell's feelings about Fowler.

Boswell was still fuming as he walked out of the Lindell AC
bar, where he had had a few drinks. Boswell couldn't hold his
liquor very well, and he was spoiling for trouble.

Bob Allison, the Twins' outfielder, followed him out of the
bar and tried to calm him down; and Boswell took out his fury

on the innocent outfielder. Allison, his hands in his pockets, talked earnestly to Boswell when the pitcher suddenly turned on him, knocked him down, and continued to pummel him.

Someone called into the Lindell AC bar, where Martin was having a drink himself, and Billy was out in a hurry.

"All right, you two!" he yelled, trying to separate Boswell from Allison.

Billy grabbed hold of Boswell. Boswell ripped off his shirt, getting free of his manager; then went after Billy himself, hitting him twice, once in the temple and once under the heart.

Boswell had made his second mistake.

"I had to go after him," said Billy, and he did. "I nailed him with several hard punches to the body, then hit him with a right to the head. He bounced off a wall and I caught him coming in with another right, which knocked him out."

Billy came out of that fight with black-and-blue marks on his body and he needed seven stitches in the knuckles of the right hand that had done in Boswell.

Boswell wound up in the hospital, where they stitched up a number of cuts in his face.

Billy sent Boswell home. He wasn't going to have the pitcher show up in the ball park looking all battered up.

"No, I don't want an apology from him," said the Kid. "I just want him to pitch his best when he comes back to the team."

In a few days Dave Boswell came back to the Twins, and by the end of the season he had become a twenty-game winner for the first and only time in his career. And, with the twentieth-win ball in his glove, he rushed into the dugout, gave his manager, Billy Martin, a bear hug, and planted a big kiss on the Kid's forehead.

"He went flakey," said Billy Martin, but he loved the gesture. It was a fitting touch to a great season, the Kid's first season as a big-league manager. The Kid had proved that he had the ability to gather a group of twenty-five assorted, diverse players, mold them into a team; inspire them, handle them, and bring the best of baseball out of them and win a championship.

Billy Martin, as so many had predicted, brought home a winner. The Twins, who had finished in seventh place in 1968, wound up the 1969 season under the leadership of Billy the Kid with a record of 97 wins against 65 losses and the championship of the Western Division of the American League. The year 1969 was the first one in which the major leagues split the teams into Eastern and Western divisions. Billy Martin had to lead his Twins against the Eastern Division champions of the American League, the Baltimore Orioles, to battle for the American League pennant.

It wasn't a good playoff series for Billy Martin and his Twins. The Orioles were extended in the first two games of the series, but they won both, in extra innings. They took the third game in a walk, 11–2, for a clean sweep and the American League flag.

It was hard for Billy to take the defeat, as it always had been and would be, but there could be no doubt about the success he had accomplished with the personnel he had inherited. He had done such a magnificent job that he was edged only by Ted Williams for the Associated Press American League Manager of the Year award by the close vote of 113 for Williams, 102 for Billy.

When Calvin Griffith called Billy into his office after the playoff, Martin fully expected that he was going to be asked to sign a contract for 1970, and perhaps there would be a sizable increase in his pay envelope. He was mistaken on both counts.

Griffith hemmed and hawed and, suddenly, Billy realized that the owner of the Minneapolis Twins was going to fire him.

The Kid was astonished.

"Did I do what I promised? Did the team win?"

Griffith nodded his head in approval, but that didn't temper Billy's fury.

He accused his boss of allowing the front office to criticize

him in front of the ball team, particularly when Martin wasn't
around. He accused Griffith of all but abetting the action of
the front office and, certainly, of not stopping it.

"You do what you like," said Billy Martin, and he walked
out of the office.

"As far as I can see, I'm unemployed," he said to the newspapermen.

A couple of days later, Griffith made it official. The reaction
of the press and the fans was immediate and loud. The papers
ran editorials condemning Griffith's action. The fans swamped
the radio stations and the newspapers with their protests, and
there was a wholesale cancellation of 1970 season tickets to the
Twins' ball park.

Griffith found it necessary to explain the firing of the winning manager who had increased the attendance at the Twins'
games, as well as the coffers of the owners of the Twins, and
had brought the Twins a division championship.

He charged that Billy Martin got into too many fights; that
he allowed the players to play poker at high stakes, as much as
five hundred dollars in the pot each deal; and, finally, he accused Billy of failing to adhere to club policy and not following his direct orders.

Billy's response was simple, direct, and sometimes revealing.

"I never started a fight, but I've never pulled back from a
fight, either.

"The pots in the poker games were never more than fifteen
or sixteen dollars, and only the players with the big salaries
were allowed to sit down at the game. We kept the small-
salaried guys out."

And for good measure, he hinted at the fact that Calvin
Griffith, for all his piety, sat in on those games from time to
time.

As for club policy and club guidelines, that meant he would
brook no interference from the front office on the way he ran
the team.

"Billy can charm the hell out of a crowd," said Calvin
Griffith. "But he ignored me."

"He was looking to fire me," said Billy Martin. "If it wasn't playing cards, it would be that I showered with the team and not in my own room. That's too much communication for them, eating, drinking, having a good time with the men. I was fired for overcommunicating. There are managers who are fired for undercommunicating. If they want an excuse, they can find it. No one is kidding me!"

No one was kidding Billy the Kid, but he was out of a job. He'd be out of a job all of 1970.

"It was the loneliest year of my life," said Martin.

Lonely years last a long time, but even the loneliest comes to an end.

Billy managed to keep himself occupied. The Grain Belt Breweries had him working in their public-relations department, speaking at dinners and luncheons mostly. He did a sports broadcast program twice a week for two Minneapolis radio shows and operated as a special assistant to the station's president. He campaigned for Bob Short, owner of the Washington Senators, in the race for the governor's office in Minnesota.

He was busy enough, but it wasn't baseball. Without baseball he was a fish out of water, in the wrong place, doing the wrong thing. He was restless, irritable, and sometimes he would be hit by the terrible depression that used to plague him.

Billy was eager to get back into baseball, but his reputation as an independent, volatile, and often ornery character didn't help. Front offices like their managers agreeable, amenable, quick to follow their wishes and execute their commands. Billy the Kid didn't fit the picture. The label with which George Weiss had tagged him, "troublemaker," had stuck. His battles, physical and other, with the Minnesota brass, which had been aired far and wide in the press, didn't encourage the other front offices in the game to rush for his services.

Still, there were two factors with respect to Billy Martin's presence on the diamond that the big brass could not ignore: He made winners out of losers, as he had demonstrated both in Denver and Minneapolis; and he brought crowds into the ball parks. He was too much of an asset to any club to be ignored forever, to be ignored for too long.

In 1971, Billy the Kid was back in the game.

October 10, 1978. Billy signs autographs at Penn National Race Track in Grantville, Pennsylvania. Billy, who plans to resume his post of manager of the Yankees in 1980, expects to watch the World Series on TV. (A.P. *photo*)

"You're Fired." That line's from one of the most unique TV commercials ever made. At left is Yankees owner George Steinbrenner with Yankees manager Billy Martin. They're shown on July 14, 1978, filming a TV commercial for the Miller Brewing Company. In the commercial Billy and George become involved in a mock argument about the beer and, by script, Steinbrenner tells Martin, "You're fired." Billy replies, "Not again, George."

August 2, 1975. Sharing a light moment in the dugout at Shea Stadium, New York, for Yankees Old Timers' Day are Whitey Ford, Billy Martin, and Mickey Mantle. Billy appeared this day as the new manager of the Yankees and was greeted with a standing five-minute ovation by the packed crowd at Shea Stadium. . . . Mantle, Ford, and Martin were known as "The Three Musketeers" when they played together on the Yankees from 1950 to 1956.

October 10, 1977. George Steinbrenner, principal owner of the Yankees, shows clenched fist to manager Billy Martin, who laughs at remark by Steinbrenner in Royals Stadium in Kansas City. The Yankees had just beaten the Royals for the American League championship.

August 10, 1977, at Yankee Stadium. Yankees manager Billy Martin congratulates Dick Tidrow on saving Ron Guidrey's win over Oakland.

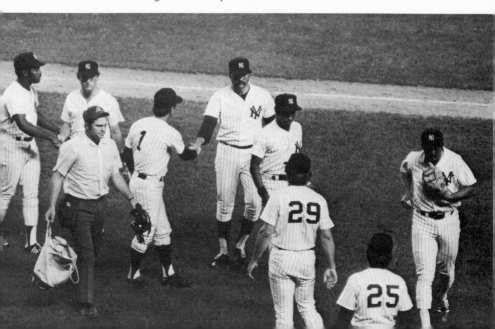

CHAPTER EIGHTEEN

The Detroit Tigers

THE DETROIT TIGERS FINISHED FOURTH IN THE EASTERN Division of the American League in 1970, twenty-nine games behind the division-leading Baltimore Orioles.

"People who pay to see us play," said a veteran Tiger, "are being gypped. We're not worth the admission price."

Jim Campbell, general manager of the Detroit club, was desperate. The Tigers were torn apart by dissension just two years after winning the World Series. Their great pitcher Denny McLain, who won 31 games in 1968, was suspended from baseball for his involvement in a gambling business. Catcher Bill Freehan had written a book that caused a great deal of animosity among the players.

Campbell didn't wait till the end of the season to get in touch with Billy Martin. Billy was the man, he figured, to put some life into what was definitely an old and tired ball club. Al Kaline, Norm Cash, Dick McAuliffe, Jim Northrup, Billy Freehan, and Willie Horton, the big guns in the Tiger attack, were all over thirty. So was Mickey Lolich, their ace pitcher. The team needed a complete overhauling and a new manager.

Campbell offered Billy a one-year contract for sixty-five thousand dollars. He promised Billy a free hand, no interference from the front office. As for the much-publicized Billy Martin temper, well merited, Campbell said, "What am I going to do, hire a man for what he is, and then try to change him? I think his temper is definitely one of his assets. It's like anything else, you have to keep it under control, and Billy knows that."

Billy Martin, pleased with Campbell's attitude, the salary offered him, and exuberant about getting back to the game he loved, and as a manager, said, "It just goes to show you how the good Lord takes care of you."

During the winter, Billy traveled around the country, personally visiting the twenty-five men he expected to make up his 1971 roster.

He talked frankly and at length to the great Tiger star, thirty-six-year-old Al Kaline, suggested that Kaline could prolong his career by playing first base, and Kaline agreed to try the position. Billy visited Gates Brown's supper club in Detroit, shot a game of pool with Brown, and promised Brown, the Tigers' No. 1 pinch-hitter, that he would get a lot more work in '71. He talked with every player and emphasized that he would be in their corner at all times. He stressed the need for team play and cooperation. His manner was so forthright and sincere and spirited that every player contacted could sense a new spirit, a tremendous turnaround in Detroit, that the club could go all the way and win under their new manager.

"I never heard a manager talk like that," said Mickey Lolich. "He talked about how the Tigers were going to play aggressive ball. He would use the hit-and-run, the suicide squeeze, and that we'd be the runningest team in baseball. He said he would treat the players fairly and would respect their rights and would back them to the hilt in any front-office argument.

"That guy Martin made me want to get up and start pitching right then and there. He was an inspiration. I think he's gonna give us a winner."

At a Detroit party for the press, Joe Cronin, president of the American League, officially welcomed Billy back to baseball.

"See this tie and this suit?" he said. "Martin paid for these with his fines the last time he was in the league." Then, more seriously, "He's a manager who inspires men around him. He's good copy for the press, and he knows how to go in fighting for his team."

"I hope Cronin remembers those accolades next summer," responded the Kid. "The World Series has been a habit with me. I like to win. I've always been on a winning team. Besides,

I promise not to punch the traveling secretary, club president, or anyone else, and I'll keep out of the alley at the Lindell AC."

Billy was good copy. The traveling-secretary allusion was, of course, to the battle with Howard Fox; it was in the alley at the Lindell AC that Billy had fought Dave Boswell and sent Boswell to the hospital.

On the first morning of spring training in '71, Billy spelled things out for the entire Tiger camp.

"I'm the leader," was the way he began. "When I see something wrong in the field, I'll tell it to you when you get back to the bench. And I get mad. And I'm not a good loser. If anybody in this room thinks I'm a good loser, they're kidding themselves. I'm a very, very bad loser. I've never heard of a good loser. I think that winning is the ultimate. I'm going to lose sometimes, and I'll accept it as a man. But that doesn't mean I enjoy losing. When I lose, it takes something out of me, and I can't eat or get to sleep for losing. When we lose a ball game, I don't want to hear any music in the clubhouse. I want you to think about why we lost.

"I want you to take pride in being a member of this Tiger club—and you do your part, I'll do my part, and we can go all the way."

Casey Stengel, the grand old man of baseball, was around and visited the Tigers' camp.

"You better do what he says," he advised them all, young and old, "or he'll knock you on your butt."

The Kid had his men hustling from the start. They were running and stealing bases, despite the fact that the team was slower and the players older than the average big-league team.

As the season opened it was obvious that the Tigers, with much the same personnel as in the dismal '70 season, were a more aggressive team. The older players—Al Kaline, Jim Northrup, Willie Horton, and Norm Cash—showed the younger players they had caught the "Martin spirit," and whenever they got on base, they were a threat to steal second, third, and even home. The Tigers kept hustling and winning and kept within striking distance of the division-leading Baltimore Orioles.

In early September, the Tigers, at one point eleven games behind, made their run for first place, and in successive days closed the gap to five games by beating the Orioles five straight times. But the spirited drive was too late and Baltimore repeated as division champions by winning their last ten games.

Mickey Lolich had his greatest season, winning 24 games while losing 14; Joe Coleman won 20 games; Norm Cash drove out 32 home runs, and 37-year-old Al Kaline and 39-year-old Gates Brown slugged the ball at a near .500 clip during the last month of the season. The Tigers as a team topped both leagues in home runs, driving out 179, and finished in second place in the Eastern Division.

It was a spectacular comeback for the Tigers, and as a reward manager Billy Martin had his contract extended through 1973 with a sizable increase in salary.

Billy Martin had done everything Jim Campbell had expected and more. Billy was especially delighted and satisfied to bring in an improved Tiger team. There was too a tremendous personal satisfaction in the Tiger comeback, for Billy never forgot that, thirteen years before, this was the same ball club that had released him as a player in 1958. It was a great comeback for Billy. He had taken a bunch of older players, "has-beens," back from mediocrity to a respectable position in the American League.

The Tigers of '72 were pretty much the same club as the 1971 team, but now they were a year older. They were still the "old men" who sportswriters predicted would wilt with the heat of summer. Nobody expected them to beat the Orioles—nobody but Martin, who had infused his players with a gung-ho spirit that gave them a feeling of invincibility. It was a spirit that only a Billy Martin could instill in a once seventh-place team.

The Kid platooned his men, gave the older players a rest

when they needed it, then rushed them back into the lineup to pinch-hit, and they delivered.

He needled and argued with Jim Northrup, and Jim, fighting mad most of the year at "that feisty son-of-a-bitch" Martin, responded by having one of his finest years. He soft-soaped Norm Cash, and the slugging Cash blasted out twenty-two home runs. He kidded Willie Horton, and Horton responded by driving out eleven home runs when they were needed the most. He bullied some, needled others, talked kindly to other players, always getting the most out of his men. Casey Stengel had said that Martin knew his psychology and knew how to use it. The result was a Tiger club that battled throughout the year in a close race for the 1972 Eastern Division championship.

Throughout the long, hot summer, the Tigers scrapped and clawed, and as the race continued into late August, the experts predicted they would fade, because so many of their regulars were over thirty. But the inspired Tigers did not fade. Woody Fryman, a cast-off pitcher, won ten straight games, Eddie Brinkman set a record at shortstop in playing errorless ball for the last fifty-six games, while Al Kaline, Mickey Stanley, and Norm Cash bolstered the attack as the Tigers came driving into Boston for the last game of the season, needing a victory to win the division title.

Once again it was their pitching ace, Mickey Lolich, with help from Fryman holding the Boston Red Sox to a single run, while Al Kaline drove out the game-winning home run, that gave the Tigers the title.

In his third year as a major-league manager, Billy Martin had won his second division championship.

Grinning like a Cheshire cat, yet wet-eyed, a very happy Billy Martin sat in the clubhouse and said, "The first thing I did when the game was over was to look up and say, 'Thank you, Lord. What a wonderful evening!'"

In the clubhouse with everybody celebrating the victory, Billy looked around at his players: Al Kaline, Dick McAuliffe,

Ed Brinkman, Jim Northrup, Norm Cash, Willie Horton, the Mexican Aurelio Rodriguez, catcher Duke Sims, Lolich, flutter-ball artist Joe Niekro, and all the others.

"It's the players," he said, "who decide if we win or lose. They get the credit. The manager just pulls the strings."

There was a streak of humility in Billy the Kid, though he didn't show it very often.

The playoff for the American League championship against the Western Division champions, the Oakland Athletics was one of the most dramatic baseball series ever played; it was a classic struggle between a club of "old" men against a club of young stars. Oakland was favored. They had won their division title for the second straight year, and had some of baseball's finest young players.

Catfish Hunter, Vida Blue, and Rollie Fingers held the Tigers to six hits in the first game of the playoffs to beat Mickey Lolich, but it took the A's eleven innings to eke out a 3–2 win. Blue Moon Odom turned back the Tigers with just three hits in the second game, and Oakland needed just one more victory to take the American League banner.

Billy the Kid may have been down, but he wasn't out. Back in Detroit, after the two losses on the coast, he insisted the Tigers were still in the series.

"We don't give up. We didn't get this far to lose," he hollered and cajoled in the clubhouse. "We're here to win, and we will!"

The Tigers responded. Joe Coleman shut down the power of the A's while Bill Freehan hit a double and a homer for Detroit; as pitcher Coleman shut out the vaunted Oakland attack, the Tigers walked off the field with their first victory of the series, 3–0.

It was Catfish Hunter against Lolich again in the fourth game, and at the end of the ninth inning it was 1–1. Oakland scored twice in the tenth, but the Tigers were not finished. With everybody including the sportswriters ready to concede the flag to the A's, the Detroit hitters came alive and scored

the three runs to win the game. The battle for the American
League flag had come to one sudden-death game.

The Tigers scored first in that final game, with a run in the
first inning. It wasn't enough. The A's came back with one in
the second and one in the fourth. Billy Martin had lost his battle for the pennant by a 2–1 margin.

Billy took the loss hard. He should have been elated, taking
a team of washed-up old men to the playoffs. He got a raise
and his contract extended to 1974 for his efforts. Nothing,
however, could comfort him for that loss to the A's, unless he
could avenge it; and, looking ahead, Billy the Kid saw little
possibility of that happening in the near future.

No one needed to tell him how old his players were. He
needed young blood, and the Tigers' farm system was not providing his needs. Besides, the Kid felt that, despite Campbell's
promises, he was getting too much interference from the front
office. Campbell and Martin were no longer buddy-buddy.

Age and several injuries began to take their toll at the beginning of the 1973 season. Al Kaline injured a groin muscle.
Mickey Lolich lost five of his first seven games. Eddie Brinkman, at shortstop, was not handling the ball well, and the slugging Willie Horton was not hitting and was benched.

Campbell didn't like Billy's act in benching Horton and
called the player and the manager into his office. Billy threatened to quit the club because of what he labeled constant
front-office interference. He actually walked out but was
quickly enough talked into returning to his job the next day.

Willie Horton was to say, later, "I'm a better player because
of Billy Martin. He motivates a club."

However, as good as he was at motivating a club, Billy
couldn't wave a magic wand and pump new energy into players
fast approaching their fortieth birthdays. The Tigers, however,
battled furiously and managed to climb into first place, but in
mid-August on a western road trip, they fell into third place
after losing six games in a row. Billy could get no replacements
for his fading veterans, no help from the farm system.

The team was going nowhere, and Billy took out his frustrations wherever he could. He blasted the Detroit farm system for failing to come up with bona fide replacements. He took on Campbell. He took a couple of verbal blasts at Bowie Kuhn, baseball commissioner, and at the league president, Joe Cronin. He took it out on the umpires, particularly for the way they allowed pitcher Gaylord Perry of the Cleveland Indians to doctor up the baseball illegally and throw the spitball.

No one ever did prove that Perry doctored the ball, but Billy Martin was convinced of it. In retaliation, and certainly out of frustration, Martin announced that two of his pitchers, Joe Coleman and Fred Scherman, would use the spitball, by way of protesting the freedom with which Gaylord Perry was permitted to use his "illegal" pitch against the Tigers.

The Kid was immediately suspended for three days by the president of the American League, Joe Cronin.

On the third day of that suspension, at the end of August 1973, Billy Martin was fired.

"I yield to no man in my admiration for the job Billy Martin did—between the foul lines," said Jim Campbell. "But he is an individualist, not an organization man. He became a threat to the efficiency of our organization."

Duke Sims, the Detroit catcher, said, "They were looking for an excuse and they found it."

Al Kaline was shocked. "You can't knock his statistics," he said of Billy.

Joe Coleman said, "It's a tremendous shock to everybody."

Joe Coleman, as well as Fred Scherman, later took the blame for throwing spitballs.

"All Billy did," they said, "was to back up his players."

Billy Martin said, "My record speaks for itself. What happened is typical of what has happened to me everywhere I've managed. I'm a perfectionist. I want to win. And along the way I step on some toes. I do things that make some people mad. But they don't stop to think I may be right and they may be wrong.

"Apparently developing a winning team and drawing people into the ball park isn't enough for the front office. I've done it twice and now I've been fired twice."

This time, however, Billy the Kid was not going to sit out of baseball for an entire year. As a matter of fact, just three days after he had been fired, Bob Short, the major stockholder of the Texas Rangers, gave Martin a new uniform and another ball club in another town.

CHAPTER NINETEEN

To the Texas Rangers

THE TEXAS RANGERS, WITH WHITEY HERZOG AS THEIR MAN-
ager, were at the bottom of the league in 1973. At the tail end
of September they had won only 47 games, while losing 91.

"I thought I was hired to build for next year," said Whitey
Herzog. "We could have won more games, I'm sure, but I
thought the future of the club was more important than winning now. I guessed wrong and I got fired."

Herzog didn't guess wrong. Bob Short would have hired
Billy Martin to take over his club no matter what Whitey had
done with the team.

"I'd fire my grandmother," said Short, "if I had a chance to
get Billy Martin."

And Billy Martin: "I like to work with someone who knows
Billy Martin." Billy had worked for Bob Short in his unsuccess-
ful campaign for the governorship of Minnesota. "And Bob
Short knows me," said Billy.

And the Rangers: "Herzog got a raw deal, but winning is
what it's all about, and Billy has always been a winner."

The problems facing Billy Martin as he took over a totally
demoralized Ranger team were seemingly insurmountable. The
pitching staff consisted of pitchers who were inept and who
could not win. There was not a single name pitcher on the entire roster of the club. The Rangers pinned their hopes in '73
on the strong right arm of eighteen-year-old David Clyde, a
local boy, a rookie just out of college, and a tremendous attraction. But Clyde just didn't have the experience. The Rangers'
infield play was sloppy, the outfield as inept. It was a team that
had to cope with player ineptness and financial problems at
the same time. Consequently, they finished 1973 with a 57–105

record. But Billy's optimism, his drive, and a few dozen victories would take care of all those problems, said the Kid.

There wasn't much he could do about turning around the Rangers in the last month of the '73 season, but the gloves and bats and balls were barely packed for the winter when the Kid was sounding off on what the Texas team was going to do in '74.

"We'll be contenders for the American League West pennant next year," he said of the team that had had the poorest record in baseball its past two years.

"I not only believe it," he said, "I'm staking my reputation on it, and my baseball reputation means a lot to me. I believe I can do it, and I believe I can do it with basically the people who are here. In players like Jeff Burroughs, Toby Harrah, Vic Harris, Dave Nelson, and some others, we've got a young ball club. One or two key players, a few good breaks, and we'll shoot for the championship. People are laughing at us now, and they will continue to laugh when I say we'll be in contention next year."

Talk like that, to the press, had to have a positive affect on the Rangers.

"Losing is just like winning," said Billy Martin. "It becomes a habit. These guys are tired of losing. I can see that. They lost a lot of one-run games on just foolish mistakes, or because our pitchers can't throw strikes, and they come back into the clubhouse totally dejected. But you wait till next year and see the kind of hustle and drive these Rangers put on. A couple of pitchers, some good infield plays, a couple of home-run hitters like Burroughs and Nelson, and the Texas Rangers will be right there on top.

"In spring training, I'm going to show them how to win," said Billy. "When they see the program I've mapped out, the strategy we're going to use, they are going to believe they can win. Winning isn't that difficult, if you know how. I know how. I got that winning spirit from Casey at Oakland and with the Yankees, and when I coached and then managed the Twins

they were winners. I won at Detroit, and now the Texas
Rangers are going to learn how to win."

Optimism is contagious, but it isn't enough to develop a
winning ball club. There had to be some important personnel
changes. And there had to be a lot of work with what Martin
considered was potentially a sound pitching staff.

"The pitching staff doesn't appear that bad," was the con-
sensus of the sports media. "But that's on paper. On the field,
they've been ridiculous."

For the most part, the Rangers' pitchers were rookies, strong
and hard-throwing.

"We know their arms are good," said Billy Martin. "So we'll
go from there."

The pitchers Billy inherited were Jim Merritt, Sonny Siebert,
Jackie Brown and Bill Gogolewski. The youngsters were the
fireballing Jim Bibby, Steve Dunning, Lloyd Allen, Pete Bro-
berg, and David Clyde, all fast-ball pitchers and all with control problems.

"There's more to pitching than a good arm," said Billy Martin. "You've got to find out what's in the pitcher's head, what's
in his heart, and what's in his soul."

Billy made some drastic changes in spring training, and
slowly but surely the Rangers began to believe their driving,
optimistic manager. Mike Hargrove, a twenty-four-year-old
rookie who had never played ball in high school or in a year at
college, caught Martin's eye. Billy kept him on the roster and
Hargrove wound up as the Rookie of the Year.

The Rangers got a tremendous boost when Billy signed veteran pitcher Ferguson Jenkins when the Cubs dropped him.
Jenkins went on to turn in a remarkable 25–12 record for the
Rangers in 1974, winning the Comeback of the Year award as
well as being the mainstay of a very thin corps of Ranger
pitchers.

Martin had an intuitive feeling about baseball players, decided that Elliott Maddox did not hustle for him, and so he
sold Maddox to the Yankees. This was the second time Billy

had gotten rid of Elliott. He had done it initially when he traded Elliótt from the Tigers to Washington. Maddox never forgave Billy and played his heart out against any team Martin managed.

Billy Martin later admitted he had made a mistake in trading Elliott Maddox, but there were few other errors in 1974 as the Rangers played in the now familiar Billy the Kid style and surprised the league by surging into first place on May 11.

Jeff Burroughs, who batted at a .301 clip for Billy Martin, hit 25 home runs, and batted home 118 runs, said of the Kid, "He hates to lose and when he does he lets you know about it. He gets real upset when you do dumb things, mentally. After a game you lose, he's angry, and you figure if he's going to be mad, let's bust our butts a little more and win. It's all psychological. It's the believability of the manager. Some managers don't mean it. Billy Martin does."

The Rangers played an inspired brand of baseball, the way Billy Martin wanted them to play, hustling, running, and battling. There were the usual number of brushoffs at the plate and the usual number of melees on the field, with Billy the Kid right in the middle of every skirmish on the diamond. And the Texas team concluded its first successful season in history, coming in second, only five games behind the Oakland A's, with a record of 84 wins, 76 defeats.

Once again, Billy the Kid had demonstrated that he could take a mediocre team, a cellar team, a losing team, and turn it into a winner. The Associated Press voted Billy Martin Manager of the Year for 1974.

During the winter of '74, Billy the Kid was already predicting that the Rangers would win the American League pennant in 1975.

"A lot of people laughed last year, too," said the Kid, "when I said the Rangers were winners. But I guess the little Dago must know what he's talking about."

Billy Martin was happy. He had good reason for it. He had done a magnificent job with the Rangers and the job had been fully recognized by the front office, the fans, and the press. In addition, he had, as a bonus, his old pal Mickey Mantle close by, in Dallas, where Mickey was operating as vice president of an insurance company, and Mickey was on the sidelines most every day, rooting and lending his good counsel.

There was the new house the Rangers had provided for Billy near the Rangers' ball park, where he was comfortably settled with his wife, Gretchen, and his ten-year-old son, Billy Joe.

He loved that boy, Billy Joe, and would take him to every home game and sit Billy Joe on the bench next to him.

"It's so exciting, that kind of love," said Billy Martin, who had always craved to love and be loved.

He had found a permanent home for himself and his family and was for once in his life at peace with himself and the world.

"I think I'll be staying here for the rest of my career," he said.

But nowhere do situations and circumstances change more rapidly and abruptly than they do in baseball. The year 1975 was going to prove to be one of anguish for Billy Martin, then suddenly open a great and unbelievable new chapter is his tumultuous career.

Bob Short, the Rangers' owner and a personal friend of Martin's, was hard pressed financially and finally had to sell his share of the Texas Rangers to young Brad Corbett, a plastic-pipe and chemical executive who now became the major stockholder in the club. But it wasn't Corbett who gave Martin any trouble, not for a while anyway. It was Elliott Maddox.

Maddox sounded off to the press, calling Martin a liar.

"He promised me a shot as a regular when he came to the Rangers, then he dumped me," said Maddox.

"I never liked his makeup, his laziness, his flakiness," came back Billy. "When I sold him to New York, I was doing him a favor, keeping him in the big leagues. He has one good year and he becomes a big mouth."

Words turned into nasty action. In a spring-training game between the Yanks and the Rangers, Jim Bibby of the Rangers hit Maddox on the shoulder with a fast ball. Stan Thomas threw a beanball at the Yankee outfielder. The Yankees, of course, retaliated, Mike Wallace throwing a couple of beanballs at Dave Nelson, and soon both teams were on the field battling each other, with Billy in the center as usual.

"I think Martin has an ego problem," said the Yankee pitcher, Mike Wallace.

Billy the Kid disclaimed responsibility for the beanballing incident and the resultant scuffle.

"They brushed Maddox off because they know he gets scared to death when someone comes close."

The beanballing continued throughout the season, with Maddox the special target whenever the Rangers met the Yankees.

"Maddox wants to get hit so he can cry," said Martin. "What he needs is a good ass-kicking."

But Maddox was comparatively a minor problem for Billy Martin in 1975. The Rangers weren't performing. They weren't winning. They were losing. And Billy the Kid waxed more and more vituperative as his team kept slipping and falling behind in the league standings.

He wore his frustration on the tip of his tongue and blasted away at everyone in sight, his players, the umpires, the front office, and the press. He began to lose the confidence of his players, and their loyalty, as well.

"It's never his fault," said one of the Rangers. "He has to blame somebody. He's gotten to think we screw up just to get him where he hurts."

Brad Corbett had defended Martin at the meetings of the Rangers' stockholders. There were some brushes with the front-office staff even in '74. Billy wanted to send David Clyde, the eighteen-year-old fast-ball hurler, down to the minors for seasoning, but Clyde was drawing the crowds, and the general manager, Dan O'Brien, rejected Martin's request. Billy threatened to quit, then had second thoughts and stayed on.

Then there was the battle with Burt Hawkins, the Rangers' public-relations man and traveling secretary. Hawkins' wife, at the suggestion of the wife of the club's president, Bobby

Brown, brought up the idea of organizing a Rangers' wives' club. (Dr. Bobby Brown, by the way, was the same Bobby Brown who played for the Yankees when Billy joined them.) Billy said that baseball was a man's business and he didn't want any women messing into it. He vetoed the plan.

He did more than that. He got into a word battle with Hawkins about it and slapped him as they were coming into Arlington on a chartered plane.

The incident on the plane became public. Billy apologized. Bobby Brown announced that Billy was on probation. Nothing more happened.

Nothing would happen to Billy Martin, whatever his differences with the front office, in 1974; he was a winner, and bringing home to Texas a winning club. It was different in 1975, with a losing club and dissension in the ranks more and more obvious.

Shocked by the obvious team dissension and inept play, Brad Corbett called every member of the team individually, and privately discussed the situation.

"There are differences between Billy and the young players, and they feel Billy is a detriment to the team," he said, after completing his investigation, but he made no demands on Billy and took no action.

The showdown between Billy Martin and the front office had to come, and it came in the middle of July, with Billy the Kid engineering its dramatic conclusion.

Billy wanted to pick up catcher Tom Egan, just released by the California Angels. The general manager, Dan O'Brien, didn't think it would be a smart move.

Corbett backed his general manager.

"We've got enough of those kinds of veterans on the payroll," he said, and Billy lost his cool completely.

He ranted, he fumed, he yelled at the general manager, he yelled at Corbett. Then, in a fit of temper, he threw the five-hundred-dollar watch Corbett had given him for a Christmas gift and smashed it against the wall.

That afternoon, Billy said to the press, "This place is a country club. I'm not allowed to control my players. They want a yes-man here. You can't win ball games if you're a yes-man."

About Corbett, "He knows as much about baseball as I know about a pipe," spat Billy the Kid. "One year in baseball and he's a genius."

Brad Corbett, understandably, fired Billy the Kid immediately. And Billy wept as he said his good-bye to the team, and the newsmen as well.

"I brought Texas a winner," said Billy the Kid. "I brought them a million fans. I brought them some real major-league baseball. I'm happy for that."

The players kept their mouths shut.

"No comment."

"No comment," was a rather devastating comment on the way the Rangers felt about their fired manager.

One of them did say, "Have you noticed that whenever Martin gets fired, the fans and the press scream but the players are remarkably quiet?"

When Billy was asked his plans for the future by the newsmen, he said, "I don't know. I love the game. Baseball is my life but at this very moment I feel like telling the game to shove it."

But Billy the Kid didn't tell the game to shove it and, in little more than a week, he was wearing a New York Yankees' uniform, the No. 1 on his shirt, not as a player again, but as the new manager of the greatest franchise in the American League.

The Rangers finished the 1975 season in third place, a rather remarkable record in view of the discord. In 1976 they dropped to a dismal fifth place.

CHAPTER TWENTY

Billy's Dream—
Managing the Yankees

SHIPPING MAGNATE GEORGE M. STEINBRENNER III, OUT OF Cleveland, Ohio, and a number of his friends, bought the New York Yankees in January of 1973 for ten million dollars from the CBS Television Network.

At a press conference to announce the purchase of the Yankees on January 3, 1973, Steinbrenner said, "I'll stick to my business of building ships and leave the baseball to Lee MacPhail and Mike Burke."

A few weeks later, Steinbrenner introduced the rest of his partners, including Gabe Paul, who as general manager of the Cleveland Indians had just traded Graig Nettles to the Yankees. Mike Burke announced, "Gabe will stay with us a couple of years, handling the acquisition of players, and then to close out his fine career retire to Florida."

Shortly thereafter Mike Burke resigned as president of the Yankees when he realized that Steinbrenner and Gabe Paul would be running the team. Burke in turn was appointed president of Madison Square Garden.

CBS had paid thirteen million dollars for the club in 1964 and had managed to lose eleven million dollars in nine years as the once-proud, imperious, rude, bullying perennial champions now languished in the second division and fans lost interest in the team and their players.

Steinbrenner intended to make money with the Yankees. He also intended to bring the championship, long missing in New York, back to Yankee Stadium.

Steinbrenner had been a star hurdler, as well as a fine halfback at Williams College. An Air Officer at Lockbourne Air Force Base near Columbus, Ohio, he was a significant wheel in

organizing a successful sports program there. After leaving the
service, he coached football and basketball at St. Thomas
Aquinas High School in Columbus. He was assistant football
coach to Lou Saban at Northwestern University in 1955. In
1956 and 1957 Steinbrenner was backfield coach for Jack
Mollenkopf at Purdue University. Steinbrenner was a part
owner of the Chicago Bulls basketball team, owned a horse
farm in Florida, and had a great love for baseball.

He was addicted to winning as much as Billy Martin was addicted to winning.

When, in 1974, the Yanks lost out in the battle for the Eastern Division title two games back of the Baltimore Orioles,
Steinbrenner, determined to win a championship for New
York, outbid several teams to sign Jim "Catfish" Hunter, the
best pitcher in the American League, to a five-year contract for
the then astronomical figure of $3.5 million. It was generally
agreed among the sports experts that, with Catfish in a Yankee
uniform, the Yankees were a shoo-in for the championship.

The sports experts were wrong. The Boston Red Sox were
running away from the rest of the Eastern Division of the
American League in 1975 while the Yankees were going nowhere.

Originally, Steinbrenner had tried to sign Dick Williams,
the successful Oakland A's manager, to manage the Yanks, but
Charley Finley, owner of the A's, set up a variety of legal en-
tanglements and prevented the deal that Steinbrenner wanted
badly. He settled on Bill Virdon, a surprise choice for the Yankee job. Virdon had been in the National League for twenty
years as a player, coach, and manager, and had been voted
Manager of the Year by the Associated Press in 1973. But Virdon didn't deliver the results Steinbrenner demanded.

Steinbrenner, a demanding, forceful executive, used to having things develop the way he wanted them to develop and ac-
customed to success in all his ventures, began to look around
for another man to manage his club. It didn't take long for
him to find that man. Obligingly, the Texas Rangers fired Billy

Martin late in July of 1975, and Steinbrenner directed Gabe Paul, president of the Yankee organization, to get him.

Steinbrenner knew all about Billy's reputation, his battles on the field, off the field, his battles with the front office, but he was sure he could handle the Kid. More importantly, he knew that Billy, like himself, had the drive to win, and that three times he had turned losing teams into winning clubs. He had to have Martin.

Gabe Paul had a little difficulty contacting Billy. The Kid, his wife, Gretchen, and his son, Billy Joe, were fishing somewhere in Colorado. Gabe finally caught up with him near Denver, and they had a long talk. That was all. Gabe Paul had offered Billy the job and a contract, but the Kid wasn't quite ready to accept the offer. He wanted to talk it over with Gretchen and Billy Joe. He had really meant it when he had said, "Baseball can shove it."

That was on a Wednesday. On Friday afternoon, Billy called Gabe to say that he was ready to take the Yankee job; and the contract, which stipulated a paycheck of about $75,000 annually for the Kid, was signed the next morning.

Bill Virdon was out and Billy Martin was the new Yankee manager.

The official unveiling of the Kid as the new manager of the New York Yankees took place, dramatically, on Old Timers' Day, August 2, 1975, at Shea Stadium, the temporary ball park for the Yanks while Yankee Stadium was being reconstructed by New York City for about $100 million.

It was difficult to suspend disbelief at the Yankees' twenty-ninth annual Old Timers' Day on August 2. The Yankees had done their best to evoke the glorious decades of the forties and fifties. All the colorful regalia of baseball's premier dynasty was on display. Draped over the green outfield façade were the faded pennants and championship flags of yesteryear: 1941 Yankees World Champions, 1942 Yankees League Champions, 1943 Yankees World Champions, 1947 Yankees World Champions, 1949 Yankees World Champions, 1950 Yankees World

Champions, 1951 Yankees World Champions, 1952 Yankees
World Champions, 1953 Yankees World Champions, 1955
Yankees League Champions, 1956 Yankees World Champions,
1957 Yankees League Champions, 1958 Yankees World Champions. Mrs. Babe Ruth and Mrs. Lou Gehrig took their ritual
bows from the stands. Mel Allen, the old Yankee announcer,
called the play by play of the Old Timers' game.

But the old-timer who drew the most attention, that day,
wasn't Joe DiMaggio or Mickey Mantle or Whitey Ford. He
was a stocky, feisty former second baseman, Billy Martin, who
that morning abruptly replaced Bill Virdon as the new manager of the New York Yankees.

Forty-four thousand fans cheered as each of the great old-
timers of the Yankees was introduced: Joe DiMaggio, Phil Rizzuto, Hank Bauer, Whitey Ford, Mickey Mantle, others. Then
came the dramatic announcement over the loudspeakers, "And
finally, the new manager of the Yankees—No. 1, Billy Martin!"

The response was a resounding, standing ten-minute ovation.
Billy had always been a favorite among the New York fans
when he played second base for their pennant-winning teams.
They had followed the career of the fiery ballplayer, through
the years of his wandering from team to team, and they
delighted in his successes as a manager, with the Twins, the Tigers, and the Rangers. Now he was back in New York, where
he belonged.

Hopes ran high among the New York fandom. Billy was the
man, if there was a man, to bring back the championship that
had eluded the Yankees the past eleven years, since 1964.

"We've chosen Billy Martin because of the excitement he
will bring," said Gabe Paul. "We know his background. We
know his temperament, his pluses and minuses. If a guy can't
learn from the experiences of three jobs, then he's not very
smart. Billy Martin is smart."

"I'm very happy, very proud to be coming back to New
York," said Billy Martin. "It's a dream come true. I just hoped
and prayed for this opportunity. I wish Casey were here, too."

Mickey Mantle said, "Billy always belonged to the Yankees."

Whitey Ford, the former ace pitcher for the Yankees, said, "It was destined to happen. It's a true marriage. Billy was born a Yankee."

There was one Yankee who was not happy about the turn of events: Elliott Maddox.

Maddox was inactive at the moment, nursing an injured knee, after surgery.

Billy called him.

"Maybe you've heard," he said. "I'm the new Yankee manager."

"Yeah," said Maddox, flatly. There was no joy in his voice.

Afterward Billy explained his feelings toward Maddox. "I didn't think he could hit big-league pitching," Martin said. "He proved that I was wrong. He told me he wants the same thing as I want—to win. That's enough for me, we both want to win. Before he was on the other team. Now we're on the same team. I feel everything's going to be OK."

"I think we can work things out," said Maddox.

There was a more embarrassing note for the Kid in the fall of '75.

Kelly Ann, his daughter by his first marriage, was in trouble with the law at Barranquilla Airport in Colombia. She was carrying a pound of cocaine strapped to her thighs and boarding a plane for Miami when the Colombian police stopped her. She proclaimed her innocence, saying she had no idea it was cocaine she was carrying, that some casual American acquaintance, John Collins, had asked her to deliver "medicine" to a sick relative living in Florida. She claimed the "medicine" was strapped to her thighs because she didn't want it stolen. It wasn't a very good story.

She called on Billy for help. Billy hired a lawyer down in Colombia. It didn't help. Kelly Ann was sent to prison for three years.

There never had been much of a relationship between the father and daughter, after his first wife divorced him. Billy

Martin's listing in the Yankee yearbooks indicated he had but one child, Billy Joe, the boy he doted on.

But the most poignant note of all in 1975, on September 29, was one of the saddest days in the life of the newly appointed manager of the Yankees, Billy Martin, for it marked the day Casey Stengel died at age eighty-five. The great manager of the Yankees had lived to see Martin, his self-adopted son, take over as Yankee manager.

Billy Martin served as a pallbearer at Casey's funeral. "It was the saddest moment of my life," he said. "I had the utmost respect for the man. For me it was like losing a father. I remember, early in my career at Oakland," Billy said tearfully, "Casey seemed like he was grooming me for bigger things. Why does a guy take a liking to certain people? I don't know. Maybe, just maybe, he thought I was the kind of kid he would want for a son. And I loved him, too."

Despite the two dampening experiences of late 1975, Billy Martin was headed for the most exciting and happiest periods in his life.

There wasn't too much he could do with the team when he took over the Yankees in August. The players were already set in their habits and playing style, which under Bill Virdon were conservative, calm, and specifically by the book.

Virdon, a strange man, hardly ever spoke to any of his players, and when he did, it was through one of his coaches. Catcher Thurman Munson says that Virdon at one point went almost three weeks without saying anything to any player. Running a baseball team to Virdon meant setting down strict rules and seeing that everyone followed those rules.

Upon taking over the Yankees, Billy said, "I saw many things, many players and attitudes that had to be changed. I saw all those guys rise to the level of incompetence. I waited and judged them—the guys who were playing for their own averages—the clubhouse lawyers.

Despite the overall ineptitude and selfish, individual attitude of some players, Billy's presence and his feverish will to win did filter through from the very first day that he was named manager of the Yankees.

Martin's first game as Yankee manager was with the Cleveland Indians in a game that was part of the 1975 Old Timers' Day celebration and amply demonstrated Martin's uncanny ability to win a big game.

For the first five innings the game was a tense 0–0 struggle that had the crowd of forty-four thousand fans roaring with every pitch. In the top of the sixth inning the Indians pounded Yankee pitcher Pat Dobson for three runs. Another Indian base hit, a walk, and Martin trotted to the mound to halt the action.

He looked to the right and to the left of pitcher Dobson as he spoke, his shoulders hunched forward, his right hand stuck in his back pocket, just like Casey Stengel used to do. Suddenly he signaled for the ace left-handed relief pitcher, Sparky Lyle, and as Dobson slowly walked off the mound, Billy took the ball, tossed it to Sparky, and said, "Let's get them outta here, Sparky."

Sparky, who had been used sparingly throughout the season by Bill Virdon, nodded his head, faced the first batter, and then in a tricky, quick motion shot the ball over to Chris Chambliss at first base to pick off the Cleveland Indian base runner to end the inning.

With the Yankees behind, 3–0, Roy White hit a home run. Billy's first pinch-hitter, Ed Herrmann, singled home another run, and now the score was 3–2, Indians.

And now, suddenly the Yankees came alive. They were hitting and running for the extra bases, and with Billy shouting instructions, pacing back and forth in the dugout, perched on the dugout step, moving his players around like a general on a battlefield—he wanted so much to win that first game, the Yankees were moving—like a typical Martin team. Two Yankee singles and then third baseman Graig Nettles stepped in to hit.

Nettles had played under Martin at Denver. He hated Billy those first couple of weeks at Denver. His orders and constant yelling were almost impossible to stand. But then, suddenly, there was a turnaround—the Denver Bears began to win. And just as suddenly Graig began to look at Martin in a new light. And Graig began to like and admire him as a manager and friend. He played again under Billy at Minneapolis and he knew now how much Billy wanted to win this first Yankee game. And he responded with a smashing single to center field that scored the tying run. The Yankees were now fighting back, running hard, taking that extra base. Chris Chambliss came up to hit and singled home the lead run as the Yankees went ahead, 4–3. Now, with Nettles on second, Chambliss on first, Martin flashed the hit-and-run sign to Rich Coggins. Coggins vainly swung at the pitch, missed, and Nettles was called out as he stormed into third base. It was a close play, and in typical Martin fashion Graig got into a shouting, shoving match with the umpire and was thrown out of the game, again in Billy Martin style.

"The umpire said Nettles grabbed his leg while getting up," said Martin, unquestionably pleased with Graig's performance. "I asked him," continued Billy, "how else he expected my player to get up quick and argue."

Graig Nettles said, "The last time I was thrown out of a game was right after Billy took over managing Denver, when I was playing there."

When Billy took over as manager, the team's record was 53–51. Under his direction the team finished the season winning 30 games while losing 26, and winding up in third place in the Eastern Division behind the Red Sox and the Baltimore Orioles. They would do better in 1976. Much better.

CHAPTER TWENTY-ONE

A New Stadium
and a Winning Team

1976 WAS THE YEAR OF THE BICENTENNIAL, AND IN NEW YORK City as well as in many other cities throughout the nation, there were gala celebrations taking place to mark this historic event in the history of the United States.

New York City, though sorely pressed and on the verge of bankruptcy, led the tribute to the nation's birthday with a magnificent extravaganza. There was a flotilla of the world's tall ships steaming up and down the Hudson River. It was the biggest collection of ships ever assembled and the most exciting event of the Bicentennial year. Mayor Abe Beame found enough dollars in the city's treasury, with help from the federal government, to finish the job of rebuilding the once-glorious Yankee Stadium at a cost of some $100 million dollars; and the city once more began to emerge from its business and financial doldrums.

For two years the Yankees had played their home games in the battlegrounds of Shea Stadium, built for the Mets and the Jets, but now on this cool, sunny day of April 14, the Yankees were back once more at home in a new, incredible, redesigned, modern Yankee Stadium.

The first practice of 1976 in the new Stadium was over as manager Billy Martin surveyed the now empty field, as he looked out through the dark sunglasses, shielding the bright morning sun. He noted many changes. The old steel columns that used to block the view of the playing field were gone. The two-story light towers above the Stadium roof were gone, replaced by modern lighting. The dimensions of the playing field had been cut down, and the center-field fence had been shortened to 430 feet from home plate. The infield looked fast, but there was a slight rough spot that had to be resurfaced near second base, there was a slight mound in center field that needed some leveling off, and the pitching mound was off slightly. They were minor details, but Billy insisted that these minor faults were to be corrected.

Back, down below in the bowels of the huge Stadium, Billy Martin, surveying his office, looked unhappy. The place was a mess, and practically bare with a battered desk and a couple of withered-looking chairs. "I need some new furniture," he shouted. "I want a new desk, a rug to cover this cement floor, a file cabinet, and a shower head for my shower. You think they're trying to tell me something?" Billy smiled. "It's the same crap all over again. Nobody gives a goddamn about the manager."

Despite the minor annoyances, Billy was delighted with the new Stadium, the facilities; the ball club looked good out there today, everything OK. He grinned as he looked about listening to the happy chatter of the Yankees as they sprawled about the locker room. The Yankees were home once again, and he was their manager. It was all like a dream—a dream come true.

What pleased Billy as much as the new Stadium were the tremendous player trades that he and Gabe Paul, working with George Steinbrenner, were able to complete. The unholy trio wheeling and dealing with an unlimited bankroll spent more money, traded for more quality players than any team in recent baseball history.

Billy had, in constant meetings with Paul, the new Yankee president, and Steinbrenner, discussed the need for Billy's type of team. "The Yankees of old in the 1930s had a Babe Ruth and a Lou Gehrig to give them all the power. They could beat you with one big inning and they did," said Billy. "In the '40s and '50s it was Joe DiMaggio, Bill Dickey, Tommy Henrich, and Yogi who could bust a game wide open and we won plenty of pennants." He grinned as he talked, now earnestly, quietly, but determined. "In the 1960s the Yankees still came through with the greatest one-two punch in baseball with Mickey Mantle and Roger Maris. But it's a different ball game today. There are no Ruths, Gehrigs, DiMaggios, Mantles around—at least we don't have 'em. So what I'd like to do is to get quality players who can run the bases—speed is what I want. If we can get the guys to hit and run, we can bring exciting baseball back to Yankee Stadium. That's what I did at Minnesota, Detroit, and Texas, and I'll do it here at Yankee Stadium, where it all came together for me."

Gabe Paul, the new Yankee president, had been a baseball man all his life, and was known as one of the shrewdest appraisers of baseball talent in the game. He had served as general manager for the Cincinnati Reds, the Houston Astros, and the Cleveland Indians before joining George Steinbrenner and his group of investors who had purchased the Yankees back in 1974. And Gabe immediately began to instrument a series of player trades that astounded the baseball world, two years before Martin arrived as manager.

Perhaps the biggest trade in '74 occurred when Paul traded four Yankee pitchers—Fritz Peterson, Fred Beene, Steve Kline, and Tom Bussby—to the Cleveland Indians for Chris Chambliss, Dick Tidrow, and Cecil Upshaw. Elliott Maddox was obtained from the Texas Rangers and proceeded to blossom out as a .300 batter for the Yankees. Then there was the trade for Kansas City's power hitter, Lou Piniella, for pitcher Lindy McDaniel. Piniella, a husky right-handed hitter, had been the American League's Rookie of the Year in 1969. He had batted .301, .279, and .312 in his next three seasons, but fell out of favor with KC's new manager, Jack McKeon, and was traded to the Yankees in December of '73. There was the startling trade of Bobby Murcer, the hard-hitting Yankee slugger who seemingly inherited the mantle of Ruth, Gehrig, DiMaggio, and Mantle, to the San Francisco Giants for superstar Bobby Bonds.

While the baseball world rocked with the news of this latest Yankee bombshell, Jim "Catfish" Hunter, one of the greatest pitchers in baseball, had been declared a free agent by an arbitration panel, and as soon as he was officially free, the most frenetic bidding in baseball history began—some twenty-two clubs waged a furious verbal and legal battle for his services.

Finally, after some heavy wrangling by Gabe Paul and the personal friendship of Yankee scout Clyde Kluttz, the Yankees shelled out some $3.5 million for Hunter's services for a five-year period.

Now in 1976, in close consultation with Martin, Gabe Paul continued trading at a dizzy pace for the speedy, hard-hitting youngsters that Martin needed. In a trade that was just as shocking as the Murcer-Bonds deal a year earlier, the Yankees sent Bonds to California for Mickey Rivers and Ed Figueroa. The very next day another tremendous deal saw George Medich, a fine pitcher, traded to Pittsburgh for Dock Ellis, Willie Randolph, and Ken Brett. The following week saw Rudy May, Tippy Martinez, Dave Pagan, and Rick Dempsey go to Baltimore as the Yankees obtained pitchers Ken Holtzman, Grant Jackson, Doyle Alexander, and catcher Elrod Hendricks.

Now Billy had pitching depth, speed, youth, and the power he needed as he fielded a team half of whom were not Yankees in 1975.

Because of a major problem, and confusion surrounding the new basic players' agreement, club owners of both major leagues decided not to open spring-training camps until the existing problems were solved. The camps remained closed for several weeks, but informal workouts were conducted all over the country until Commissioner Bowie Kuhn ordered the camps opened.

When the camps did open Billy Martin spent a great deal of time with rookie second baseman Willie Randolph, shortstop Fred Stanley, and the new center fielder Mickey Rivers. Hour after hour, day after day, Billy was at second base working with Randolph and Stanley. Billy showed Willie how to move to second base, take the toss from the shortstop, pivot properly, and then whip the ball over to Chris Chambliss at first.

For a decade the Yankees had been looking for a second baseman like Bobby Richardson, and Martin himself during the 1950s, and until Randolph came along they had found no one. Randolph, with but thirty major-league games under his belt, was the most impressive youngster in camp. He hit .292

and ran the bases well. As a result he won the coveted James P. Dawson Memorial award as the best rookie in the Yankee camp, and as the Opening Day game with Milwaukee approached, Martin was confident that he had the finest Yankee team since 1964, the last year the Yankees won a pennant.

As the season opened, sportswriters predicted that the Boston Red Sox would repeat their championship form of '75, while the Baltimore Orioles would finish second. There were numerous writers who predicted that the Yankees would be extremely lucky to finish fourth in the race for the Eastern Division flag.

There was something wrong with their calculations, for the Yankees featuring a lineup that included Chris Chambliss, first base; Randolph at second; Fred Stanley, shortstop; Graig Nettles at third base; Roy White, Mickey Rivers, and Oscar Gamble in the outfield, and a starting rotation of first-rate pitchers, including Catfish Hunter, Ed Figueroa, and Dock Ellis, with Sparky Lyle and Dick Tidrow as the relievers, looked as formidable as any club in the league.

In the opening game of the season, a cold day in Milwaukee, the Brewers spoiled Catfish Hunter's thirtieth birthday by pounding out a 5–0 victory. Hunter complained to Martin that the pitching mound had too much slope, and Billy stopped the game to protest. But that did not help. Hunter allowed the Brewers but six hits, but could not stop Milwaukee's great slugger, Hank Aaron, who drove in three of the Brewers' runs. The following day the Yankees pulled out a 9–7 victory over the Brewers, and then there was a day to remember.

On Thursday, April 15, 1976, the first game was played at the "new Yankee Stadium," glistening white outside and royal blue inside, with 54,100 fans on hand, including former heavyweight champion Joe Louis, Frank Gifford, Mickey Mantle, Joe DiMaggio, Phil Rizzuto, Whitey Ford, Mrs. Babe Ruth, Mrs. Lou Gehrig, and six members of the 1923 Yankee team that had opened the Stadium, as former Yankee second baseman Bobby Richardson delivered the invocation. Then the game got under way.

Don Ford of the Twins drove out a home run with two men on base in the first inning, and the Twins scored another run in the third, but the Yankees came back with a run in the third, four runs in the fourth inning, and six more in the eighth. Oscar Gamble drove in three runs with a single, double, and triple, while Mickey Rivers drove out three hits to wrap up an 11–4 victory. After the game, Martin beamed. "We had to break in the new Stadium right," he said.

The next day the Yankees again bombed the Twins, 11–0, as Ed Figueroa allowed Minnesota just six singles, and then the Yankees ran up a string of five straight victories to climb into first place in the Eastern Division on April 20 with an 8–3 record.

The Yankees then went on a tear, winning twenty of their first thirty-two games, and by the middle of May sportswriters suddenly started to notice the Yankees. It was easy to see that they were a new Yankee team, a hustling, base-stealing, aggressive, and exciting team. They were, in fact, a Billy Martin team.

When the league champion Boston Red Sox came to the Stadium on May 20 for a four-game series, Martin placed tremendous emphasis on this series. "Boston's still the team to beat," he said.

The Yankees were in first place in the league standings, while the Red Sox languished at the bottom, but it was still early in the pennant race, and every club was in the race.

The Red Sox-Yankee series had always been close, hard-fought battles, and this series was no exception. As Billy Martin sent his charges out onto the turf at Yankee Stadium, they were ready for the Sox. Pitcher Ed Figueroa of the Yankees and Bill Lee of the Red Sox battled each other in an exciting, tense struggle for six innings until Lou Piniella, charging like a high-powered locomotive, rounded third base and headed for home, after singles by Nettles and Otto Velez. Lou suddenly realized that Dwight Evans' great throw would beat him to the plate; nevertheless, he kept on coming and smashed into catcher Carlton Fisk at the plate.

Both men went down hard and suddenly they were battling each other, fighting, punching, clawing as players from both teams came charging into the melee. Billy Martin rushed into the center of the combat area, but was kept busy trying to separate the battlers. For once in his life, he was trying to keep the peace. Pitcher Bill Lee, realizing his pitching arm had been injured, charged at Graig Nettles; Graig, a battler who had played under Billy on three different teams, promptly smashed Lee to the ground with a savage left to the jaw.

When hostilities were stopped and play resumed, Carl Yastrzemski smashed a home run with a man on base to give Boston a 2–1 lead. In the eighth and ninth innings Yaz homered to win the game for the Sox, 8–2.

Tempers somewhat cooled the next day as the Yankees pounded the Red Sox pitcher for fifteen blows as Kerry Dineen, a new face in the Yankee lineup, cracked a single to left with two men on base in the twelfth inning to win a tense game, 6–5.

On Saturday, before a Stadium crowd of forty-five thousand, the Yankees and Red Sox played another extra-inning game, with Catfish Hunter winning a 1–0 shutout, allowing the Sox just three hits. On Sunday, the Yankee fans jammed into the Yankees' new stadium some 52,994—the largest crowd in years, to watch Jim Rice ruin the day for the Yankees, who went down in defeat, 7–6.

After the game Yastrzemski, the great Red Sox slugger, full of admiration for Billy the Kid, said, "Billy Martin has taken mediocre ball clubs and made them good. Now he's taken a good ball club and made it great. They double-steal with two outs. They try to take an extra base in the bottom of the ninth. It's hard to play catch-up ball with a ball club like that."

"We like each other," said the great Yankee catcher, Thurman Munson. "We have fun together. In the past there were factions on this club, cliques, a division on the team. Some guys didn't like each other. There were times when guys choked in games or worried more about themselves than the team. But this ball club is fun. This ball club is together."

Chris Chambliss, the star Yankee first baseman, lauded his boss for his loyalty. "Billy sticks up for you," he said. "He stands by you."

Roy White, a veteran Yankee, spoke of the easy relationship between Billy the Kid and his players. "When I've had things on my mind, I could talk to him. You can talk with him man to man."

One afternoon, Graig Nettles called to his manager, "Hey, Billy, you can't see the ball, it's getting so dark. Can't you get them to turn the lights on?"

"Sure," said Billy; and to the empty spaces in the park, he yelled, "Turn on the lights!"

And, pronto, the lights came on.

Nettles just stood there and grinned.

"I always knew you thought you were God," he said to the smiling Billy. "You didn't have to prove it."

But no season for Billy the Kid could be without its dissensions, without its anguish, no matter how well his club was playing, no matter how high the morale of his players.

There was the scene with pitcher Doyle Alexander. Billy had yanked him out of the game after he had given up four runs on seven hits in four innings. The move seemed reasonable enough, but Doyle came off the mound fuming.

"They were horseshit hits!" Alexander yelled at his manager. "My arm's as good as it was the last time."

"I decide how good your arm is," spat Billy the Kid, "not you!"

He locked the clubhouse door and kept the sportswriters out after that scene in the dugout.

"A player never talks back to the manager," he said to the entire assembled squad, his voice sharp and taut, "not in front of the other players."

His eyes were fixed on Alexander.

"I've an office and a door that's open for that. If anyone does that again, talks back to me in front of any other player,

I'll kick the crap out of him right there in front of the whole team."

For once, Billy the Kid had controlled himself. Only a few years back, maybe only a few months back, he would have torn into Doyle Alexander with his fists, not words, and right in the dugout.

Then there was the Sparky Lyle situation. Sparky, one of baseball's finest relief pitchers, had been in Virdon's doghouse and had seen little action for the entire previous year. Billy had used Sparky from the moment he had taken over direction of the Yankees. But Sparky had been ineffective on the mound for several games, and back into the doghouse he went. Lyle wasn't happy about the situation. Nor was Billy Martin. He valued and needed Sparky. Sparky was his ace fireman. But Billy didn't know quite how to handle the situation.

"I'd sure like to have Casey around now," he said, "to ask him how he handled it, not using a guy. I wish Casey had lived ten more years."

Mickey Rivers was a vexing problem for a while, too.

Mickey liked to have his wife along on the Yankee road trips and sulked when Martin bawled him out about this. Billy felt that wives interfered with the concentration of his players, hampered their game.

"They're worrying about their wives, where they are, how they are, instead of keeping their minds on the ball game."

There was no problem with Elliott Maddox. Maddox spent most of the season on the disabled list. Nor was there any overt difficulty with the front office; George Steinbrenner did have Billy uncomfortable and worried with his constant phone calling and second guessing, a prelude to the more anxious days Billy Martin was to experience with time.

After one game, Steinbrenner called a meeting of the Yankee pitchers and dressed them down for their collective performance. This was the kind of "interference" by the front office that raised the Kid's hackles and had led to the battles with the brass and the subsequent firings of Billy the Kid by the Twins, the Tigers, and the Rangers. But Billy, grown perhaps a bit more mellow, more tolerant, but certainly wiser, kept his mouth shut, at least for the moment.

Steinbrenner was a frequent visitor in the clubhouse after games, and Billy took that, too. But he wasn't happy.

There were two days' running when George Steinbrenner had Dick Williams sitting with him in his box at the Stadium. Billy began to wonder whether he shouldn't have pursued a more vigorous course with the front office.

It was August 4 and the Yankees had returned from a disappointing road trip. They were nine games in front of the pack, but Billy was very unhappy as the Yankees had lost six of the past seven games. A couple of matters disturbed Billy. There was the matter of a new contract that George Steinbrenner had not discussed or even mentioned.

And the presence of Dick Williams, recently fired as manager by the Angels, in the Stadium, sitting with Steinbrenner, didn't promise much peace of mind for the Kid. Everybody knew how the Yankee boss felt about Williams, and rumors began to mount in the press.

As for Billy, he had been fired before, after bringing home winners. Much as he hated to think of the possibility of being separated from his beloved New York club again, he knew it was a distinct possibility, and he didn't feel too good about it.

In September, however, with the Yankees leading their division by 11½ games, Steinbrenner made the inevitable decision.

"Billy and I have a rapport that few people have," said the shipping magnate. "I have seen him go to Minnesota and Detroit and Texas and do a hell of a job and get fired. I don't think that will happen here, because I know Billy. I know how to get along with him."

Steinbrenner offered Billy a two-year contract. Billy insisted on a three-year contract, and finally signed a new contract at about a hundred thousand dollars a year.

Steinbrenner had a word of caution.

"In a winning organization," he said, "no one is indispensable. That goes for the manager and it goes for me, too. I think Billy understands that."

There was cause for a clubhouse meeting on the afternoon of September 24, after the Yankees lost the opener of a double-header to the Tigers at Tiger Stadium, 3–0. "It was no chewing-out session," said Billy. "We just talked about the need to bear down. We needed one more win to clinch the pennant."

The Yankees stormed out of the clubhouse and proceeded to blast the Tigers into defeat by the score of 8–0. Grant Johnson allowed but five hits and struck out five, while Graig Nettles delivered his thirtieth homer as the Yankees blasted Tiger pitchers for eleven hits.

Most of the players sat in a little restaurant in Detroit after the game listening and waiting for the Baltimore Orioles' game to end. And it did, when Luis Tiant and the Boston Red Sox defeated the Orioles, 1–0. And the Yankees were the American League Eastern Division champs. It was the end to twelve years of waiting, playing through season upon season, until the Yankee victory over the Tigers and the Oriole loss.

Once again, Billy Martin had brought home a winner.

CHAPTER TWENTY-TWO

Winning the Playoffs

THE DAY BEFORE THE OPENING OF THE PLAYOFFS FOR THE American League pennant between the Yankees and the Kansas City Royals, Martin had some words for the press.

"I'm cutting off all players' telephones in Kansas," he said. "I told them it was to keep them away from crank calls. Actually, it's so their girlfriends can't call them, since their wives will be with them. Some of them are so dumb their wives could sneak into town and catch them in bed with a broad. That's why I made the rule that they had to check with me before they could bring their wives on the road."

Billy the Kid was feeling good. He'd been in playoffs twice, and lost them twice. This time the sportswriters were predicting a Yankee victory, and the Kid was all confidence. The Royals, who had been in a terrible slump at the end of the season, losing nine of eleven, had backed into the Western Division championship, and it looked like an easy romp for the surging Yankees.

The Yankees won the first game, 4–1, amid some of the most vituperative jockeying that emanated from both benches.

The Yankees, behind the magnificent pitching of Catfish Hunter, played super baseball. Hunter, who failed to win twenty games during the regular season for the first time in six years, had the Kansas City hitters at his mercy. He allowed the Royals only five hits, while the Yankees pounded Larry Gura, an ex-Yankee, for four runs. Third baseman George Brett, who carried on a verbal battle with Billy Martin, committed two costly errors in the first inning that led to two runs, and the Yankees were in command the rest of the way.

Larry Gura said, "Martin was calling me names, typical low class. Nothing you can print."

"I got on Brett because of some of the things he said to the papers," said Billy Martin. "If Brett wants to fight me, I ain't looking for it, but I ain't backing away, either."

While Billy was being a little less harsh about Gura, a cop came into Billy's office.

"Mr. Martin," he said, "we just want you to know that we've received a threat. Some nut, probably, says he's going to blow up the stadium."

This was the kind of setting built to Billy the Kid's order.

"This is no goody-goody-two-shoes party," he said. "This is for a major-league pennant. We're out to win any way we can."

The next day, as the Yankees went down to defeat, 7–3, Billy was involved in a running fight with the angry Royal fans, trading insult for insult. But the Kid was in a good mood. He was all smiles to the belligerent fans as he walked back from the mound to the dugout after relieving starting pitcher Ed Figueroa; he even blew kisses to the crowd.

The third game was played in Yankee Stadium, and the Yankees took it, 5–3. One more win and Billy Martin would have his first major-league pennant. He elected to send Catfish Hunter to the mound to bring in that much-coveted American League championship, but Catfish didn't have it that day and the Royals evened the series at two apiece, winning 7–4. The pennant, an entire year's work, was down to a single game.

Billy was tense. He had George Steinbrenner on his back calling him, meeting with him, suggesting numerous lineup changes. That didn't make him feel any easier. Maybe he should have given Hunter an extra day of rest? He wondered about starting Figueroa. Figgy had been hit hard in the second game. Perhaps he should rest him for another day? He became more certain of it when the Royals banged home two runs off starting pitcher Figueroa in their half of the first inning.

The Yankees came back to score a pair of runs in their half of the inning. The Royals scored once in the second; the Yankees twice in the third. When New York scored another pair in the bottom of the sixth, Billy Martin began to relax for just a few moments. It was just as well. George Brett slammed a home run off relief pitcher Grant Jackson in the top of the eighth inning with two men on. The score was tied. It was now a tense, exciting, heartthrobbing game with the championship riding on every pitch.

With the momentum seemingly on the side of the Royals, it looked like Billy was going to lose his third try at an American League pennant. But the Yankees weren't out of it yet. Something of Billy's contagious drive must have rubbed off on his team. Instead of returning to their dugout dejected after Brett's home run tied the score, the Yankees came in hollering and cheering. This was one game that wasn't going down the drain. This was one game they were going to win.

In the top of the ninth, the Royals got two men on base but couldn't score.

In the bottom of the ninth, Billy Martin recited a Hail Mary prayer, something he had never done during a baseball game. Chris Chambliss, the first Yankee batter, stepped up to the plate.

The fans, in their frustration, littered the field with garbage as the Royals took the field. The garbage had to be cleared before play could be resumed. It was cleared and then Chambliss swung at Mark Littell's first pitch. It was a fast ball, waist high, and Chris drove into the ball with all the power in his strong body and hit the ball nearly 420 feet over the right-field fence. Home run! The Yankees were American League champions for 1976!

Martin jumped for joy, like the kid at heart he was, while Chambliss struggled around the basepaths, fighting his way through the thousands of fans who poured out onto the field, deliriously happy. He managed to touch second base just before the fans tore it away. He fell among a horde of fans between second and third, clambered back onto his feet. It took a corps of teammates and the police to get him to home plate; he never made it. Home plate had been uprooted.

Police finally cleared a way for Chris to dive into the club-house doorway.

It was the first pennant the New York Yankees had won since 1964.

Chambliss was a hero.

Billy Martin was a hero. Every Yankee player was a hero.

On the playing field thousands of people screamed for joy. In The Bronx, Brooklyn, Queens, Staten Island, all over Manhattan people danced in the streets. In the bars all over New York strangers toasted each other and cheered themselves hoarse.

In the clubhouse Billy Martin, choked with emotion, a bottle of champagne in his hand, stood between Mayor Abe Beame and silver-haired Cary Grant. "I've never been as excited as this," Martin shouted. "Not even when I got that big hit in the '53 series."

George Steinbrenner pushed his way to Billy's side and threw his arms about the happy Martin. "I'm very proud of you, Billy," George said.

"I wish Casey were here to see it," Billy said. "This was his pennant."

Among the celebrants in the happy Yankee clubhouse was a Cleveland sportswriter. Billy, a bottle of champagne in either hand, spotted him and shouted, "Hey, who's that guy on that Cleveland radio show who's always riding me? I got a message for him I'd like you to print in your paper. Tell him to kiss my Dago ass!"

Billy laughed so hard he almost fell down. It was the most joy he had ever known in his life.

Billy Martin was riding high. The kid who was born on the other side of the tracks, from West Berkeley, California, the street fighter, the dead-end kid, banished from the Yankees and bounced around six teams, had returned as manager of the Yankees and led those same Yankees to the championship of the American League. If ever an ego built on the foundations of a sense of inferiority could be justified, Billy the Kid had done just that. If ever a man needed to be loved by the multitude, Billy the Kid had that, too. But there was just one more goal the Kid had to attain before he was to be completely satisfied, primarily, with himself: the championship of the world. That goal, in 1976, was to be denied him, and in the most devastating manner.

It was a bitter-cold day that first day of the World Series at Cincinnati's Riverfront Stadium, October 9, as Billy Martin led his Yankee squad in a final showdown against Sparky Anderson's powerhouse Cincinnati Reds. The Reds were the National League champions. They had a fine pitching staff and an awesome lineup of power hitters in Johnny Bench, George Foster, Joe Morgan, Pete Rose, Dan Driessen, Tony Perez, and Cesar Geronimo. It was a lineup that terrorized the National League all season as the Reds romped home to win the Western Division title by 10 games over the Los Angeles Dodgers. In the playoffs the Reds overwhelmed the Philadelphia Phillies, sweeping the Phils in three straight games for the National League flag.

Down in the clubhouse, Billy Martin had just posted his Yankee lineup for the first game of the World Series when a reporter asked him what he thought about the betting odds that established the Reds as the big favorite. "I don't care what Nick the Greek thinks," Martin said. "I never met a Greek who was a smart baseball player. All that bullshit about how great the Reds are and how great the National League is, that's not going to bother me. Back when I played with Whitey and Mickey, we used to beat them all, and we'll do it again."

Billy was excited, nervous, but confident as he led his team onto the field and surprised everyone with his choice of Doyle Alexander as the Yankees' starting pitcher. The experts thought that Ken Holtzman, who was 8–3 over the Reds, would start for the Yankees. "I picked Alexander," Billy explained, "because he has an unorthodox delivery that could bother the Reds."

Don Gullett, the Reds' starting pitcher, was very fast as he struck out Mickey Rivers, Thurman Munson, and got Roy

White on an easy ground ball. In the last of the first, peppery Joe Morgan drove out a home run to give the Reds a 1–0 lead. The Yankees scored in the second inning on a sacrifice fly by Nettles, but the Reds came right back to add another run to take a 2–1 lead after three innings. Cincinnati added another run in the sixth inning and two more in the seventh to give them a 5–1 lead over the Yankees, as Don Gullett pitched strongly to hold the Yankees in check, and the final score was 5–1 Cincinnati.

In the second game, on Sunday, Catfish Hunter, the Yankees' ace, faced the ex-American Leaguer, Fred Norman. Hunter seemed uncomfortable on the pitching mound and complained several times to the umpires, but they did nothing about the extreme slope of the mound. At any rate, Hunter was not at his best at the opening, allowing eight hits and three runs in the first four innings. Finally in the fifth inning Catfish settled down in the cold weather—it was below forty degrees—and he was the Catfish of old allowing the Reds but two scattered base hits for the rest of the game.

In the fourth inning the Yankees came to life as Billy Martin exhorted Thurman Munson to start something—and Munson did, with a sharp single to center for the first Yankee hit. Chris Chambliss also singled, and Munson scored New York's first run on a single by Nettles.

A single by Willie Randolph and a double by Fred Stanley produced a second Yankee run in the seventh. Roy White then singled as Fred Norman was replaced by relief pitcher Jack Billingham for the Reds. Billingham induced Munson to force White at second base as Stanley scored, and the Yankees were even at 3–3.

The score was still 3–3 in the bottom of the ninth inning as Hunter got the first two Cincinnati batters out, and then Ken Griffey hit a slow grounder to Fred Stanley at short. Taking plenty of time for the throw, Stanley nevertheless threw the ball into the Reds' dugout for a two-base error. Tony Perez then lined a single to left and it was Cincinnati 4–3 over the Yankees.

In the press room after the game an angry Billy Martin faced a horde of interviewers and offered this explanation for the two straight losses. "You have to have a little luck to win," he said, "and we haven't been getting it. The Reds hit bloopers for base hits and score runs. We hit line drives and they catch them."

As the Series shifted to Yankee Stadium, Martin was tense and moody at this point. He had endured tremendous pressure all season long, and it was intensifying by the hour. The Kid expressed the hope in an interview before game No. 3 that the natural turf at Yankee Stadium would help the Yankees rebound from two straight defeats. "Dock Ellis is a sinker-ball pitcher," Martin said, "and I purposely held him back for this game because he'll be more effective on the grass than on the artificial turf."

But the natural turf and the home grounds at Yankee Stadium were of little help as the Reds scored three runs off Ellis in the second inning and knocked him out of the box in the fourth as the Reds scored another run to give them a 4-0 lead.

Yankee shortstop Jim Mason smashed out a home run with a man on base to give the Yankees two runs, but the Reds came back with two more runs and a 6-2 win for game No. 3.

The fourth game, delayed a day by rain, was featured by a Cincinnati deluge of blows that included two home runs by Johnny Bench as the Yankees went down fighting but utterly defeated by a team that had to be rated as one of the finest in baseball history.

In the ninth inning of the final game of the debacle, a frustrated, angry Billy Martin threw a foul ball, which had landed in the dugout, at umpire Bill Deegan, and Billy was immediately thumbed out of the game. The Reds had a 3-2 lead at the time, but no one in the park, not even Billy, had any hope of the Yanks pulling a ninth-inning miracle, winning the game. Final score: Reds 7, Yanks 2.

George Steinbrenner spoke to the team in the clubhouse after the game. He was not defeated. At least he didn't sound defeated.

"There're 550 major-league ballplayers who weren't in this Series," said Steinbrenner. "We'll be back."

And Steinbrenner and the Yankees would be back. No one in baseball with the exception of Billy Martin was more determined to collect the baseball championship of the world than was this hard-boiled shipping magnate.

Billy Martin didn't meet with the press until he felt he was calm enough to face them. That took at least a full half hour. When he did appear, his face was drawn thin and his eyes were red.

"Yes, I've been crying," he said. "I'm not ashamed to tell you I've been crying. It hurts my pride, my ego too, I guess, to lose like this."

There can be no doubt about Billy Martin's pride nor about his ego. Both were to play key roles in his trials, his defeats, and his triumphs in 1977.

CHAPTER TWENTY-THREE

Reggie

GEORGE STEINBRENNER WAS A DETERMINED MAN. HE WANTED a World Series championship for his New York club. He needed it for his ego, an ego that, if anything, was even greater than Billy the Kid's ego. If Steinbrenner had to, he was going to "buy the best team in baseball."

This was the year of the free agent. The Yankees outbid all other teams to purchase the Oakland A's great pitcher Vida Blue for $1.5 million and the flashy 1976 World Series winner, twenty-six-year-old left-hander Don Gullett from the Cincinnati Reds, but Commissioner Bowie Kuhn voided the Vida Blue sale, ruling that the sale of a player for that much money with no other players involved was not in the best interest of baseball.

Dismayed at Kuhn's rule but undaunted, Steinbrenner decided that he would go all out in an effort to outbid the more than twenty clubs in the market for baseball superstar Reggie Jackson, who had become a free agent. To that end Steinbrenner had dinner with Thurman Munson, the Yankee team captain, the outspoken, burly, hard-hitting catcher who was extremely popular and was well liked by the other team members. Steinbrenner wanted to solicit Munson's views as to how Munson and his teammates would accept Jackson's aggressive and flamboyant nature.

"Go get the big guy," Munson told Steinbrenner after discussing the various aspects of Jackson's play. "He's the only guy in baseball who can carry a club for a month. And the hell with what you hear about this or that, he hustles every minute on the field."

Steinbrenner immediately contacted Reggie and flew him to

New York City, where they had breakfast at the exclusive
Carlyle Hotel. There was a gourmet lunch at the world-famous
"21," where Steinbrenner introduced Jackson to some of New
York's most famous personages. Steinbrenner, who can be the
most charming man extant, wined and dined Reggie and
dazzled him with the prospects of playing for the Yankees, and
at the end of a two-day courtship handed Reggie the keys and
bill of sale for a $63,000 Rolls-Royce.

To say that Reggie was impressed would be putting it
mildly, and when Steinbrenner carelessly tossed him the keys
to the Rolls and said, "Reggie, the car is yours no strings at-
tached, whether you sign with the Yankees or not," Reggie was
overwhelmed. However, much as he was dazzled by Steinbrenner, he held off any final agreements pending a meeting
with his agent in Chicago and also to discuss the offers from
the Montreal Expos, the San Diego Padres, and the Baltimore
Orioles.

Notwithstanding all the various meetings that Reggie had
scheduled in Chicago, Steinbrenner flew to Chicago and interrupted those meetings already in session to privately talk with
Jackson once more. It was after this final meeting that Reggie
had made up his mind to play in New York for George
Steinbrenner with a reported five-year contract that called for a
$2.93 million deal.

Reggie Jackson had been an outstanding high school athlete
in Wyncote, Pennsylvania. He received thirty-one athletic
scholarship offers. Notre Dame, Michigan, and Penn State
wanted Reggie to play football for them. He had been an outstanding high school back, playing both offense and defense.
But he went to Arizona State University because he wanted to
play in their outstanding baseball program. While Reggie was
still a sophomore at Arizona State and the star of their championship baseball team, Charley Finley, the brilliant, eccentric
owner of the Oakland A's, signed Reggie for a bonus of
$85,000, and when Reggie joined the A's after his sophomore
year at college, he blossomed into one of the premier sluggers
in baseball. For eight years Reggie carried the A's through

October 17, 1977. New York Yankees manager Billy Martin gestures indicating one more win will give the Bronx Bombers the World Series Championship. The Yankees hold a three—two edge over the Los Angeles Dodgers as inclement weather forced postponement of the sixth game.

October 1978. The World Champion Yankees' ticker tape parade on Broadway as more than a million New Yorkers salute the champs. Who said New York was blasé?

February 15, 1978. At Fort Lauderdale, Florida, Yankees manager Billy the Kid Martin wearing a Western style hat greets Catfish Hunter at the Yankees' spring training camp in Fort Lauderdale as the Yankees camp opened for spring drills in preparation for the 1978 season.

New York, July 27, 1977. Yankees manager Billy Martin acknowledges a standing five-minute ovation from the fans at Yankee Stadium after he went to home plate to present the lineups for a game with the Orioles. Orioles manager Earl Weaver is to Billy's right. The Yankees came from behind to defeat Baltimore 5 to 4.

some of the most exciting, winning seasons in their colorful history, including three consecutive American League pennants and three World Series triumphs.

Reggie was going to make for a different New York Yankee team in more ways than one. He was colorful, confident, obstinate, and temperamental. He was an intelligent man, a sensitive man, a moody man, and a loner. He was particularly aware of the struggle of blacks for a respectful and respected place in the American scene. He had already accumulated wealth that he estimates at $9 million from land and real-estate trading in Arizona. He was the Most Valuable Player in the American League in 1973, led the league in runs batted in once and in home runs twice. He was the clean-up hitter on three World Series winners with Oakland. He had his sweet time in Oakland and despite the periodic grief Charley Finley handed out to him, he bided his time until he was traded to Baltimore. He made a valuable contribution to the 1976 Orioles, reporting a month late after being traded by Charley Finley. At Baltimore, Jackson held out for more money, but was still suffering intense personal shock as a result of the trade. Nevertheless, he kept an underrated Oriole team right on the backs of the Yankees, nearly overtaking them at one point. When Baltimore refused his salary demands, Reggie became a free agent.

Reggie is a very perceptive man. By his count, he has an IQ of 160. His commentary is often one-sided and self-serving, but he has an understanding and an awareness of the needs of others that few ballplayers can match, for he can never brave the protection of ignorance.

On November 19, the Yankees held a press conference at the Americana Hotel in New York to announce that Reggie Jackson had signed to play for the Yankees. Facing a horde of some 150 newsmen and a battery of television cameras, Reggie calmly explained his reasons for signing. "For a day or so after the ruling, I didn't think I would play for New York, but then George Steinbrenner took it on his own to hunt me down. He's like me. He's a little crazy, and he's a hustler. It was like trying to hustle a girl in a bar. Some of the clubs offered several hundred thousand dollars more, but the reason I'm a Yankee is that George Steinbrenner outhustled everybody else and there are certain things he said to me, and certain ideologies and philosophies that we talked about and reached an accord on. And another important thing," said Reggie, "I didn't come to New York to become a star. I brought my star with me."

This was an ego that promised to clash with the ego of Billy the Kid, and it did. It would clash, too, with several other egos in the Yankee lineup.

Later the Yankees revealed some details of the nearly $3 million contract. Reggie would receive a salary of $332,000 a year for five years, $132,000 of it deferred; a $400,000 bonus plus $40,000 a year for fifteen years for public-relations duties for a grand total of $2,660,000. Reggie also obtained a $250,000 loan at a low 6 per cent interest rate, and the Yankees paid Reggie's lawyers' and agents' fees.

When the final financial figures of Reggie's contract were made public, it caused consternation among key Yankee ballplayers, including Munson, Nettles, and Sparky Lyle.

Thurman Munson was particularly angry. "George Steinbrenner talks about loyalty. He told us to be loyal to him and he would be good to us. His loyalty went out of the window. We helped him win the pennant, but as soon as a good player becomes available, there goes $2 million or $3 million to him. But the guys who won for him see very little of it."

Thurman Munson's salary had been raised from $165,000 to $200,000. With Reggie Jackson getting $320,000, it wasn't enough for the big catcher. He let everybody around, the press and the front office, know that he wanted to be traded.

At a dinner in Hamilton, Ontario, Munson, as the guest speaker, told a dinner crowd that he had been "lied to and deceived" by Steinbrenner. The Munson story was picked up and circulated throughout the nation's newspapers. That very night at 1 A.M., Steinbrenner phoned Munson at his home in the midst of a card game with friends. He asked Thurman to fly to New York and to meet with him. The next day Munson flew into New York and renegotiated his contract, which among other considerations included a great deal of cash up front.

Reggie was received coldly and impersonally by his Yankee teammates in spring training. Not that he minded too much; he was pretty much of a loner. Reggie was interviewed by *Sport* magazine, and what he had to say about assuming the leadership of the team and his opinions of some of the other Yankees nearly blew the team apart when the article appeared in June.

But the Yankees didn't wait till June for dissension to become a way of life on the New York club. One way or another, the unity in the Yankee camp began to fall apart in spring training, and it wasn't always Reggie Jackson who was responsible, one way or another.

Mickey Rivers was fined for reporting late for practice. He fretted and fumed, sulked, was reprimanded again and again by Martin, and Mickey did not respond willingly to the criticism.

"If they don't like any of my habits," he said, "then let them trade me. The hell with their nonsense."

Sparky Lyle was most unhappy. He wanted his contract renegotiated, and if that didn't work out, he wanted to be traded.

Graig Nettles, the marvelous third baseman, despite the fact that he had previously signed a three-year contract with Steinbrenner, was very unhappy at his inability to renegotiate and perhaps add two additional years to his contract, and jumped the team. When the Yankees took the team bus from the hotel in Tampa for a game in Dunedin, Florida, Nettles was on his way back to Fort Lauderdale.

And adding to the boiling cauldron, George Steinbrenner was most unhappy because Martin kept Reggie Jackson out of the lineup during spring training, and Steinbrenner was unhappy to note the "loose" spring-training camp that Billy ran.

Billy was keeping Jackson out of the lineup in the preseason games because Reggie had a sore arm and Billy wanted to give the ailing Reggie plenty of time so that the arm would not become a chronic problem once the season started.

George Steinbrenner was on the warpath. Billy was running a loose, disorganized spring-training camp. Camp drills were not as organized and gung-ho as George thought they should be. He was an old football coach and believed in timed, precision drills, where the players moved around the field like well-oiled machines.

He thought the Yankees' camp lacked the careful, organized planning he felt that spring training called for, the kind of training camp that typified college or pro football—organization, planning, preparation, timing, precision, and discipline.

Billy had other problems; marital problems. His marriage to Gretchen seemed to be breaking up. He was living a bachelor's life with his old pal Mickey Mantle in Boca Raton.

After an ignominious loss to the Mets in a spring-training game, George Steinbrenner hit the boiling point.

The team bus, parked outside the clubhouse, was taking on Yankees for the ride back to camp. Next to the bus was Billy Martin's car. He had come in from St. Petersburg, and he was going to go back to St. Petersburg, in his own car.

Steinbrenner charged into the clubhouse.

"I want to see you!" he shouted at Billy, livid with rage. "I want to see you now!"

Billy turned to his boss, calm, but just for a moment.

"I want you to ride on the team bus!" yelled George Steinbrenner.

"You don't tell me where to ride, you son-of-a-bitch," came back Billy, his voice as loud as Steinbrenner's.

"Watch yourself," said Gabe Paul, who, fortunately, was present.

"You lied to me!" screamed Steinbrenner.

"You're a lying son-of-a-bitch!" came back Martin.

Steinbrenner kept yelling.

"Why aren't you using the starters? Why have you got Jackson on the bench?"

"Don't tell me how to manage my ball team!" said Billy the

Kid. "I'm the manager and I'll manage how I want to manage!"

"I ought to get rid of you," threatened Steinbrenner.

"Fire me right now, if you want to," the Kid challenged. "But leave me the hell alone!"

Steinbrenner didn't fire him, not just yet, but the tone had been set and the die cast.

There were a couple of bright spots in that '77 spring-training session. The Yankees acquired Paul Blair, sending a discontented Elliott Maddox to Baltimore. Bucky Dent, an outstanding shortstop, was acquired from the Chicago White Sox in a trade for Oscar Gamble. That was it.

"This has been the worst spring training in my whole history in baseball," said Billy Martin.

The regular season produced no visible change among the Yankees. The dissension continued to mount, and it was evident enough as they lost eight of their first ten games and were settled uncomfortably at the bottom of the standings in the Eastern Division of the American League.

George Steinbrenner was on the phone constantly, wanting to know what the hell Martin was doing about the slump, and Billy, fighting hard to control his team of egotistical all-stars, became desperate as turmoil erupted regularly. He began to worry—and to drink.

Sparky Lyle and Ed Figueroa were fined $100 each for sleeping through a Steinbrenner "pep talk" in Kansas City.

Lyle and Mickey Rivers were fined $500 each for passing up an exhibition game in Syracuse.

Catfish Hunter criticized Martin's selection of pitchers and the rotation of the pitchers on a Milwaukee radio show.

Ken Holtzman called Steinbrenner a "damn fool" for paying $165,000 a year to him for bullpen duty.

Mike Torrez, a new Yankee pitcher, criticized Steinbrenner for insulting him with a meager contract.

And Billy Martin was beside himself at his inability to control Jackson and to satisfy Steinbrenner. There were additional arguments with Thurman Munson and Lou Piniella. It was almost too much to bear, and Billy began to lose weight. He was not eating, he couldn't sleep, and he began to drink heavily. On May 16, just before a game with the White Sox in Chicago, Billy became very sick and almost passed out. During the middle of the game the team doctor noticed Billy's pallor and actions and ordered him to check into a hospital immediately.

Billy refused and just clamped his jaws tight, shook his head in evident anguish, and sat through to the end of the game. Although the Yankees at this stage of the pennant race were but one game behind the division-leading Red Sox, Billy felt that his world was coming apart—he had seemingly lost control of his team, and he would be fired.

Several days later, at Toronto, Sparky Lyle walked into the trainer's room and to his surprise saw Billy stretched out, eyes closed, on the trainer's table. "If he hadn't had a little color in his face," said Sparky, "I would have thought he was dead. He'd been subjecting himself to some terrific punishment. I think the bullshit from the front office was finally taking its toll."

On June 9, the Yankees returned to Yankee Stadium to face the Milwaukee Brewers after a nerve-wracking road trip that included eleven games in a row in five cities. There were five tiring plane trips to the cities, and then trips to another hotel in another city in the middle of the night. There were constant packing and unpacking, irregular sleep, poor meals at odd hours, and two days of 100 degree heat playing in Texas.

"It was the worst trip I've ever been on," Roy White said. "By the fifth inning of the Texas game, I was like dead. The thirty-four-ounce bat felt like thirty-four pounds. My legs felt heavy. Even the ball felt heavy."

Yet the Yankees, despite the horrors of the trip, won seven games and lost four. They left New York at the end of May a game and a half out of first place and returned to New York at the top of the Eastern Division by a full game.

The most remarkable of all the Yankee success stories of the year was Ron Guidry. In spring training with the Yankees in

1976 Guidry seemingly was near the end of his baseball career. He had spent five long years chasing the dream in towns like Johnson City, Fort Lauderdale, Kingston, West Haven, and Syracuse, all the steps on the way to the big team, the Yankees. His success was only fair, with nineteen victories and twenty-one defeats, but the hope and the promise were still burning.

Then suddenly in the spring of 1976, at the age of twenty-five, he was ready to give up the dream; he was a failure as a pitcher.

"I had a good spring-training period," Guidry remembers, "and Billy told me that I was going to be a backup man to Sparky."

The idea suited Guidry fine. Backup to Sparky Lyle, the best relief pitcher in the American League, was not such a bad job. At least it was New York, and the big leagues. Guidry's heart was full and he had big plans about living in New York with his wife and a promising big-league future at last.

But when the season started, there was no room on the roster for Ron Guidry, and it was back to Syracuse.

Ron's reaction to the news was, "Hell, no. I won't go back." The Yankees said, "You're not pitching enough here. You have to go down to Syracuse, where you'll get the work you need."

"I got fed up," said Guidry. "I decided that I'd had enough. I packed up all our clothes in the car and my wife, Bonnie, and I were on Route 80, heading South, going home.

"Suddenly," Ron remembers, "we were on Interstate 80, heading South at a good clip, when Bonnie finally said, 'Ron, do you really want to give up baseball? Do you want to quit? You know you won't be happy not playing ball. Ron, don't do something you'll regret the rest of your life.'

"I thought about what she said," Ron said, "and I told her, 'OK, if you don't mind going back to Syracuse. It'll all right with me. I'll give it one more try.'"

Back in Syracuse, Guidry's performance was sensational: He won five straight games, and struck out fifty batters in forty innings. But the following spring (1977), at Fort Lauderdale, Guidry was hit hard in those early spring-training games, and once more he was on the verge of being shipped back to the minor leagues. Even those in the Yankee front office who had been high on his potential began to have doubts.

"They told me everything about Ron," said Martin, "but they never told me he doesn't look good in the spring."

The one man whose faith in the skinny, 160-pound, 5-foot, 11-inch left-hander never wavered was the Yankee president, Gabe Paul. Now he is president of the resurging Cleveland Indians, but Gabe looks back at 1977 and Guidry and said, "Some people high up in the Yankee organization wanted me to get rid of Guidry. This one man questioned Guidry's heart. I wouldn't buy that," said Gabe. "I remember one game in Syracuse where Ron came in with the bases loaded and struck out the side. That takes heart. I don't care where you're pitching."

As the 1977 season rolled on, Yankee pitchers were hit hard and often, and there were injuries to Don Gullett and Catfish Hunter. Ken Holtzman was ineffective, and in desperation Billy Martin used Guidry in relief and Ron saved a game. There was another relief chore, another save, and another, and on a night that Ron Guidry and Bonnie will never ever forget, Martin gave him his big chance, a start against the Kansas City Royals. The Yankees needed a win desperately, and Martin gave Guidry the starting assignment.

Guidry shut out the Royals, 7–0, on a night that saw the Yankees move into first place—on the arm of the skinny rookie, who pitched his first complete major-league game, allowing Kansas City but three scattered hits while striking out seven batters. At one time during the crucial game, Ron retired seventeen batters in a row. It was one of the most remarkable pitching performances of the year, and it gave the Yankees a lift they badly needed.

During the ensuing few weeks Ron Guidry started nine games and won eight in a row. Five of the games were complete games, and just as quickly as that, Ron Guidry in the space of a few short weeks, was the mainstay of the New York Yankees' pitching staff and the pitcher that manager Billy Martin would call in time and again to win the "big game."

Just at a point where things seemingly looked bright for the team, all hell broke loose. The *Sport* magazine story by Bob Ward featuring Reggie Jackson's quotes was brought into the Yankees' clubhouse. Every player had a copy and the story was being read with considerable astonishment, then disbelief, then anger, then rage.

"That prick!" said Munson.

They looked directly at Reggie Jackson, getting himself dressed for the game.

"That dirty son-of-a-bitch!"

They walked by his locker on the way to the field and made sure to take a kick at his shoes and equipment bag as they passed.

Thurman Munson, chief target in the Jackson article, said, "I can see if he knocked me in one page. But three pages! I couldn't find enough adjectives about myself to fill three pages."

Jackson had put down Munson as a crude, overbearing, and utterly unlikable guy in the magazine article. He admitted that Munson was a mean and tough competitor, and a good hitter, but charged that Thurman was overrated as a catcher. As far as being a leader, Reggie considered Thurman Munson a joke. All he had to do, said Reggie, speaking about himself, was to walk into the clubhouse and take over.

And Reggie's ego was spelled out, for all to read and resent, throughout the article.

"I've got problems other guys don't have. I've got this big image that comes before me. And I used to be respected as a black athlete. Now I'm respected as a tremendous intellect."

There was more.

"This team, it all flows from me. I've got to keep it going. I'm the straw that stirs the drink. Maybe I should say me and Munson, but he doesn't really enter into it. He's been so damned insecure about the whole thing."

And more.

"He'd try to cover up, but he ought to know he can't cover up anything from me. Man, there is no way. I can read these guys. No, I'll wait and eventually he'll be whipped. Then I'll go to him and we'll get it right."

And still more.

"I'm a leader and I can't lie down. Let me put it this way. No team I am on will ever be humiliated the way the Yankees were by the Reds in the World Series. That's why Munson can't intimidate me. Nobody can. You can psyche me. You can take me one-on-one in the pit, and I'll whip you. That's the way it is. Munson thinks he can be the straw that stirs the drink, but he can only stir it bad."

Despite the crack about the '76 World Series debacle, Reggie Jackson was a mite subdued about Billy Martin.

"He won't have to be the bad Billy Martin fighting people anymore," Jackson had said. "I'll open the road, and I'll let the others come thundering down the path."

There was still more about Munson, and more of Jackson's own ego.

"Wait till I get hot and hit a few, and I have New York eating out of the palm of my hand, Munson won't be able to stand it.

"The rest of the guys should know that I don't feel that far above them. We should be able to get along. I'm not going to let the team get divided. I'll do my job, talk to anybody. I think Billy will appreciate that."

Understandably, Billy appreciated none of it. As for the players, they just ignored him. The tensions in the clubhouse continued to grow. Something had to give, and it did, in a televised game, the eighteenth of June, in Fenway Park, Boston.

Boston was leading the Yanks, 7–4. Fred Lynn was on first base and Red Sox slugger Jim Rice at bat. Rice checked his swing but the ball hit Jim's bat, sending a short pop fly into right field. It was Reggie's ball but he started late for it; at least, he went for it so indifferently that the ball dropped for a base hit before he could get to it, and when he did field the ball, he just lazily lobbed it toward the pitcher's mound.

Rice raced into second on the poor throw. In an instant Billy the Kid, seething, was on his way to the pitcher's mound.

He signaled the bullpen for a pitcher to relieve Mike Torrez.

"I'm going to get that son-of-a-bitch," he fumed, speaking to Munson, who had joined him on the mound.

The "son-of-a-bitch" he had in mind was Jackson.

Billy signaled Paul Blair to come in; he was pulling Reggie out of the game.

Reggie had been talking to some of the players in the bullpen. The sudden roar of the crowd turned him around. He saw Paul Blair coming out, to replace him. He couldn't believe it.

As the center-field TV camera followed him all the way, Reggie charged back into the dugout.

"What did I do?" he asked Billy, completely bewildered.

Billy the Kid was off the bench to greet him.

"You know what you did!"

"Why did you take me out? You have to be crazy to embarrass me in front of fifty million people!"

Elston Howard, knowing well that there might be more than words between the player and the manager, moved in front of Reggie.

Billy cursed. Jackson cursed.

"You showed me up in front of fifty million people. You're not a man!" spat Reggie. "Don't you ever dare show me up again, you mother."

Billy's long restraint of his antagonism for Jackson broke.

"I'll show you whether I'm a man or not!" he yelled, and he charged after Jackson.

Howard tried to stop him. Dick Howser grabbed him, and Yogi Berra pushed him down on the bench and held him. Jim Wynn stopped Reggie Jackson, as Reggie turned around to meet the challenge.

"You never did like me. Billy, nothing I can ever do would please you. You never wanted me on the ball club," Reggie

Jackson shouted. "Well, I'm here to stay, so you'd better start liking me."

It was all out in the open now, and fifty million people, and maybe more, had been witness to the revelation.

George Steinbrenner was in Cleveland that day, but he had seen the entire confrontation on TV, and he wanted to fire Billy Martin immediately.

Gabe Paul calmed him down.

"You don't want people to think that Jackson is running the team."

Jackson was beside himself. That evening he sat in his room at the Sheraton Hotel in Boston sipping white wine and reflecting on the incident. Several reporters were present to talk with him. His face was a mash of sorrow and pain, and his mouth uttered many choice expletives. Then abruptly, Jackson dropped his reserve and showed all the pain in a tirade against Martin. "It makes me cry the way they treat me on this team," he said. "The Yankee pinstripes are Ruth and Gehrig and DiMaggio and Mickey Mantle. I'm a nigger to them and I just don't know how to be subservient. I'm a black buck with an IQ of 160 and making $700,000 a year. They never did like me on this team before."

Reggie was emotionally tight. The humiliation he had suffered, in front of millions, was too much for him to take.

"Steinbrenner treats me like I'm somebody. I love that man."

The tears were flowing.

"I'm a Christian and they're fucking with me because I'm a nigger and they don't like niggers on this team. . . ."

Mike Torrez, who had been sitting in the hotel room throughout the interview, watching Jackson with considerable concern, said to the newsmen, "I think that's about enough. I think you'd better go now."

One note: Billy was color-blind. WASP, Pole, Puerto Rican, Black, Jew, the only thing that mattered for Billy was whether the man could play ball. As a fact, his reputation for working well with, for living well with Hispanics, blacks, and other minorities went back to the days when he was hired for that special attitude of his to coach at Minnesota.

The morning after the confrontation in the dugout, Milt Richman, sports editor of United Press, published a story that stated that Billy the Kid was going to be fired in a matter of days and that Yogi Berra would replace him as manager of the Yanks. The story probably saved Billy his job, for the time being, anyway.

George Steinbrenner liked to deal man to man, not through the press. The UPI story made him more amenable to the arguments of Gabe Paul, Fran Healy, and Reggie Jackson.

There was a meeting of Steinbrenner, Paul, and Martin. It was the same old hash about flexibility and discipline and loyalties. Billy may have been rather quiet during the meeting but he wouldn't back down on the justifiability of his actions or anything he had said.

Then suddenly the calm, reasoned actions of Fran Healy, a rugged giant of a man who had become Reggie Jackson's friend and confidant. Healy, a six-foot-five, second-string catcher, initiated a series of meetings with Steinbrenner, Martin, Jackson, and Munson.

After speaking with Healy all Monday afternoon, listening to his calm, collected explanation, Jackson met with George Steinbrenner and then in a remarkable about-face surprisingly appealed to George not to fire Billy. Then Healy met with Steinbrenner in the hotel lobby and provided Steinbrenner with an insight into how the other players felt; then Healy met with Martin and brought Billy up to date on the various meetings. Then Billy met with Steinbrenner and George laid out in no uncertain terms the changes Billy would have to make in his attitude and behavior. Another final meeting with Martin, Steinbrenner, and Jackson and peace—for the moment—was restored.

They didn't fire the Kid.

"You guys are a finger-snapping away from firing your manager," Steinbrenner said to the men in a clubhouse meeting.

"If you love the guy so much, you'd better get on the ball and win some games. That's all I have to say."

But abruptly, in August, as the team continued to win, a remarkable change took place in the Yankee organization, both on the field and in the clubhouse, and even on the team bus.

Reggie Jackson gave up sitting up front, aloof from his teammates, and moved back into the bus to join with his teammates in an attempt at some friendly banter. There were amicable hellos and pats on the back in the clubhouse. Billy Martin was calling Jackson "Big Guy" and letting him know that he appreciated both his hitting and his fielding. And more importantly, the Yanks began to play the kind of baseball they were capable of and they began to win.

It was August 12 and less than a week since the last crisis, and suddenly it all seemed to come together. Reggie Jackson began to play inspired ball. He hit a double and a triple in the first game of a double-header against the Angels and knocked in three runs. He drove out two tremendous home runs in successive at-bats in the second game. He also threw out a runner at the plate with one of the finest throws of the year as the Yankees took two games from the Angels, 10–1 and 9–3, and ran their winning streak to five.

Hunter and Ed Figueroa pitched complete games and suddenly everything was clicking.

August 18 and the Yankees, rolling along in a drive to stand off the Red Sox, defeated the Tigers in a ninth-inning rally, 5–4. Mickey Rivers drove out three hits and scored three runs, and Willie Randolph had three hits and scored twice. The next day the red-hot Yankees beat the Texas Rangers, 8–1, for their twelfth victory in thirteen games. And now suddenly with Jackson, Nettles, Rivers, and Randolph pounding the ball, and with the remarkable pitching of rookie Ron Guidry, the Yankees seemed like they were finally "on their way to final victory."

The Yankees were the best team in baseball anywhere, in August.

In the first hundred games of the season, all the million-dollar boys could show for their effort was a 55–45 effort. But, beginning with August, they played at an .800 clip, winning 40 of their next 50 games.

Reggie Jackson hit at a .310 clip. Mickey Rivers batted an incredible .405. Graig Nettles hit .340 and collected 10 home runs. Chris Chambliss, in one 14-game period, hit .346.

Billy the Kid's team was moving at last, but Billy Martin, with the Reggie Jackson problem settled and out of the way, said, "I ask one thing of a player and that's hustle. If any player won't hustle, and shows the team up, I show the player up. I don't care if the whole world saw it. I'm not going to let television run my team."

Billy was of the opinion that the incident with Jackson at Fenway Park turned the Yanks around. Actually, it was some six weeks before that the Yankees began to fill the promise of the multimillion-dollar club.

The race for the Eastern Division crown, until the New Yorkers began to move, was pretty much of a seesaw affair, Boston and Baltimore taking the lead at one time or another, with brief appearances of the Yanks at the top every now and then. There were times when the Yankees took off on a winning streak, only to fall behind quickly with a skein of losses. And each time the club went into a spin, no matter how brief, there were rumors that Billy the Kid's tenure as manager of the New York club was all but over.

Of course, there were the usual front-office denials but, on one occasion anyway, coach Dick Howser was called in by Gabe Paul and interviewed as to the possibility of managing the Yanks. He turned the "possibility" of the job down. Only a thoroughgoing masochist would take on the job of managing a team as torn with dissension as were the Yankees.

In Baltimore for an important series with the Orioles in early July the pressure once more tightened around Billy's neck. In a meeting with Martin, Thurman Munson said Billy talked about his personal problems and became very upset. Martin confessed his inability ever to understand Steinbrenner and also expressed his personal concern for his family if he got fired. "He had signed a contract at Steinbrenner's insistence," said Munson, "which gave the Yankees a number of ways they could avoid paying him his salary. As we talked," said Munson, "tears welled in his eyes and rolled down his cheeks. To avoid having anyone see him so upset, I walked him around the block until he could regain his composure. I felt very close to Billy that day," said Munson.

By the time the Boston Red Sox came to Yankee Stadium in September for another "crucial series," the Yankees were in first place by a game and a half. The Sox were primed for this series. They had won five games in a row and eleven out of thirteen since a seven-game losing streak dropped them out of first place.

Meanwhile, the red-hot Yankees won twenty-four of their last twenty-seven games and surged to the top.

Carl Yastrzemski, the great Red Sox slugger, said of this series: "I don't understand either team. When we were behind, we played like hell. When we got in front we played lousy. The Yankees have done the same thing. It seems both teams have reacted to falling behind. But this is the big series. We've got to win three out of four or we're gone."

There were more than 55,000 fans at the Stadium as the game started, with the incredible Ron Guidry on the mound for the Yankees. The big crowd roared every time Ron had 2 strikes on a Sox batter. Ron opened the game by throwing 10 pitches in the first inning as he struck out the side. In the second inning Yaz slammed out a 420-foot triple and the Sox jumped into a 2-0 lead. It lasted until the fourth inning, when the Yankees took charge. Lou Piniella singled home the first Yankee run in the fourth inning, and in the fifth inning, Bucky Dent singled and Mickey Rivers drove out his eleventh home run of the year, to give the Yankees a 3-2 lead.

In the dugout, Guidry turned to Martin and said, "Skipper, if we can hold them the rest of the game, don't let them score, we'll win!" Then Reggie Jackson sprinted home after a Chris Chambliss double to give the Yankees a 4-2 win.

September 14 was a day and a date that Billy Martin, Reggie Jackson, and Ed Figueroa will never forget. In a game against the Red Sox, a "must win" situation for both the Yankees and the Sox, a crowd of some 54,365 people witnessed one of the most exciting, nerve-wracking, tension-filled games in many years. It was a game featured by the marvelous pitching of Ed Figueroa and Boston's Reggie Cleveland, a classic pitching duel that saw players on both teams make incredible diving one-handed catches, 400-foot outs, and the biggest crowd of the season roared on every pitch as manager Billy Martin and Boston's manager Don Zimmer used every conceivable strategy to win the game.

But the star of this classic game, a game that Bucky Dent calls "one of the most exciting games in my life," was the incredible Reggie Jackson. He made two remarkable catches in the field. Once he actually leaped halfway out of the park, leaning over the wall to spear a home-run drive. Another time he dove to the grass and just snared a line drive in his outstretched glove to save at least a double and a run.

It was o-o and the Yankees were at bat in the last half of the ninth inning as Reggie came up to hit. And now Yankee Stadium was a bedlam as the huge crowd demanded, implored Reggie to come through with a hit.

"Reggie! Reggie!" the thunderous roar reverberated throughout the Stadium. "Reggie! Reggie!" they roared.

Thurman Munson had started the cheers when he led off with a single to left, and now Billy Martin in the dugout decided that Jackson should sacrifice Munson to second. But when the Red Sox pitcher came in with a high, hard pitch for ball one, Martin decided to give Reggie the "hit away" sign. Now the count had reached three and two, and the crescendo of noise was deafening.

Reggie Cleveland came in with a startling pitch—a tremendous fast ball that was almost too low to hit cleanly. But Jackson, swinging low and underneath the ball, with his tremendous strength, golfed the pitch 430 feet into the bleacher seats in right center for a 2-0 victory that practically clinched the division title.

"When I hit the ball," said Reggie, "it was like a fairy tale. It was a tremendous feeling. You can feel everybody loving you, you can feel all the people pulling for you. When I hit it, I had the feeling I was sharing it with everybody."

And when Reggie circled the bases and touched home plate, Billy Martin was the first to grasp him in an embrace, as the rest of the Yankees simply engulfed and swarmed all over the ecstatic Reggie.

The magic number was one: One more game won by the Yankees or one loss each by the Red Sox and the Orioles would clinch the division title for the Yankees.

But it wasn't until the next-to-last day of the season, with Baltimore and Boston knocking each other out of the race, that Billy Martin's club clinched the Eastern Division title. Billy should have been elated, and to all intents he was, as he celebrated the win along with the rest of his players by dousing Steinbrenner, Gabe Paul, and every player with champagne; but the battles with Jackson, with the front office, and particularly with George Steinbrenner had taken the real joy and happiness from him. Outwardly he was happy, but deep down within he was badly hurt. He wanted to be paid for the four times they had come close to firing him. He wanted to be congratulated for holding together a team that was torn apart with dissension and personal antagonisms, and bringing them in as champions. He wanted to be paid for all the anguish and personal torture he had had to endure throughout the year.

"If I get fired," he said, still not certain he had a job with the Yankees in 1978, "I'll beat him."

The message was for George Steinbrenner.

"If he buys $50 million worth of players, I'll beat him with another club, and he knows it. If he asks me back, and if I come back, I'll make him cry."

Before the playoffs, again with the Kansas City Royals, who had repeated in the Western Division, Martin said, to a group of writers, "If we win everything, I think it's a must for George to come up with another contract. If he doesn't, I'll have to think about asking permission to talk with other clubs."

CHAPTER TWENTY-FOUR

Playoffs and World Series, 1977

THE 1977 PLAYOFFS BETWEEN THE ROYALS AND THE YANKEES was every bit as climactic and dramatic as their 1976 struggle— no less tense, no less dramatic.

The Royals started with a rush, walloping Yankee pitcher Don Gullett for four runs in the first two innings and breezing to a 7–2 win in the first game of the playoffs.

Remarkable Ron Guidry pitched a three-hitter to even the series. Mike Torrez lost the third game. "I was chopped to death," he said. Sparky Lyle came out of the bullpen in the bottom of the fourth, in the fourth game, to shut off the Royals' attack, and the series was even once again.

Again, as in '76, the battle for the American League pennant had come down to the fifth and final game of the playoffs.

Ron Guidry started. He was not effective, and at the end of three innings it was Kansas City 3, New York 1. Mike Torrez volunteered to relieve and held the Royals scoreless into the eighth inning. Lefty Paul Splittorff had held the Yanks to a single run but, when he gave up a single to Randolph leading off in the Yankee eighth, Whitey Herzog sent in his ace reliever, Doug Bird, to face Munson. Munson struck out, but Lou Piniella singled, sending Randolph to third.

With the Royals seemingly safely in command in the eighth inning, Martin, who had benched Jackson, now sent in Reggie to pinch-hit against Bird, and Reggie promptly singled Randolph home. The score: Royals 3, Yanks 2. Billy Martin explained his reason for benching Jackson.

"Two of my players told me Reggie didn't hit good against Splittorff," the manager said. "It's not a decision I'm happy

making, but I have to do it. I probably wouldn't in a World
Series, but I just have to do it now."

Billy did not tell Jackson himself that he wasn't playing. He
seldom told his players anything directly. He had one of his
coaches, Yogi Berra or Dick Howser, carry the messages. It was
something he learned from Stengel.

Manager Whitey Herzog sent in his twenty-game winner,
Dennis Leonard, in an attempt to shut the door on the Yanks
in the ninth, to wind up the series with a Kansas City victory.
But Paul Blair singled and Roy White walked. Larry Gura
came in to relieve Leonard and faced Mickey Rivers. Everyone
in the park expected Rivers to bunt, to move Blair and White
into scoring position. It was the orthodox play. But Billy Martin was never the orthodox manager, and he ordered Mickey to
hit away. Mickey responded with a sharp drive over second
base, scoring Blair. Score tied, 3-3.

Roy White, with the go-ahead run, was on third. Willie
Randolph, always reliable in the clutch, sent a towering fly to
center field and Roy White came flying home after the catch
as the Yankees went ahead, 4-3.

The Royals went down meekly in the last of the ninth, and
the game was over. The playoffs were over. And Billy the Kid
had done it again, brought in a winner, his second American
League championship in two years.

The Kid poured the victory champagne all over George
Steinbrenner.

"That's for trying to fire me!" Billy shouted.

"If I want to fire you, I'll fire you," came back George
Steinbrenner.

They laughed. Everybody in the clubhouse laughed. They
were celebrating a great victory. Underneath, the old dissensions, the old antagonisms, burned bright.

"This was a goddamn tough team to manage," said Billy to
the press. "I held them together. That man almost cost us the
pennant."

"That man" was George Steinbrenner.

And Steinbrenner, as always, had his response for the newspapermen.

"We put this team together without Billy," he said. "We got him the best players money could buy. He's crazy to take the credit for the success."

Billy drank his share of the victory party champagne, and maybe a little more than his share. Then he switched to his favorite drink, scotch. The tensions of the year had all but shattered his nerves. The Kid, who used to toss his drinks into a flower pot, was pouring them down his throat. He was drinking heavily. His appetite for food began to diminish. He was taking pills to increase it, get it back to near normal. The trials and torments, the anguish he had suffered had come close to breaking him down physically; and there were the Los Angeles Dodgers to face in the World Series.

Billy Martin, more than anyone else, with the possible exception of George Steinbrenner, wanted to win that Series, and the world championship. For Steinbrenner, it was the glory to feed his ego that was important. For Billy Martin, it was the proof that Steinbrenner needed him. The world championship, Billy was certain, would give him the ammunition to deal with Steinbrenner and Company, put him in the driver's seat, give him the edge he needed to battle against the aggressive and domineering shipping magnate.

But the Dodgers were no pushovers. The last time the Dodgers and the Yanks had played in a World Series, in 1963, Sandy Koufax, Don Drysdale, and Johnny Podres, with a bit of help from relief hurler Ron Perranoski, had whipped the New York club in four straight to take the championship. It was a humiliation that had to be repaid, and Billy, always confident, always the optimist, was sure his team was the team to take care of that little item and redeem the pride of the Yankees.

Billy sent in Don Gullett to win the first game of the Series, and Don didn't quite make it. Sparky Lyle relieved him in the ninth inning, with the score tied at 3–3. Lyle stilled the Dodger bats through the twelfth, and it was a Willie Randolph double and a Paul Blair single, sending Randolph home, that gave Billy Martin his first World Series win.

Catfish Hunter hadn't pitched a ball game for almost a month. On his last outing, September 10, he was the losing pitcher in a game the Yanks lost, 19–3. Billy chose to pitch Catfish in the second game of the Series.

Reggie Jackson voiced his objections and, as usual, for the press. He was thinking of Catfish, rather than the game. He didn't think Hunter, who had been ailing, should pitch, and that he'd be humiliated, again, before the millions of TV fans.

But Billy knew very well what he was doing. Dick Tidrow was the only man really available to him, after the torrid playoffs against Kansas City, and he needed Tidrow in the bullpen.

Ron Cey, Steve Yeager, and Reggie Smith, all hit home runs for the Dodgers, and Los Angeles had evened the Series. Billy Martin's gamble with Hunter had not paid off.

Reggie Jackson repeated his criticism of Martin.

Billy's response: "He can kiss my Dago ass."

Reggie heard that and came back with a cryptic, "If I had an ethnic origin, I'd tell him what he could kiss."

Antagonism, antagonism, antagonism.

Munson had a few words of his own.

"If I was hitting .111 [Jackson's batting average in the first two games against the Dodgers] I wouldn't be second-guessing the manager."

And Sparky Lyle: "So what else is new?"

Mike Torrez pitched the Yanks to a win in the third game of the classic, 5–3, and everyone in New York felt a little better. They felt even better when Ron Guidry pitched a four-hitter and led the Yankees to their third win in the Series, 4–2.

Reggie Jackson hit a home run in the sixth inning of that game, Billy didn't send Blair out to replace him in the late innings for defensive purposes, and Reggie embraced his manager after the game, and even thanked him for leaving him in the game.

Reggie did more than that. In the clubhouse he nominated

Billy for the Nobel Peace prize, and Billy accepted the nomination, graciously, even humbly.

Only one game away from the championship, the Yankees were all sweet talk, generous, and almost forgiving.

The fifth game proved a walkaway for the Dodgers as they clobbered Don Gullett. Reggie hit his second homer in two games. Munson hit one, too. But the Dodgers were ahead 10–0 before the Yanks could score a run, and Los Angeles took the game, 10–4.

The Yankees still needed just one more victory to win the World Series title.

Gabe Paul called a press conference. Despite the performance of Billy Martin's charges against the Dodgers, George Steinbrenner hadn't been denying stories that he was about ready to fire Billy. Gabe had to do something to counteract the rumors, if only to bring some cohesion into the ranks of the players for the last game, or games of the World Series.

"We are pleased to announce," said Gabe Paul, "that Billy Martin will continue as Yankee manager and has been rewarded with a substantial bonus in recognition of the fine job he has done. We hope this will put to rest the unfounded rumors that a change was about to be made. Billy's contract runs through the 1979 season."

The bonus was in three parts: about $50,000 in cash, an apartment rent-free, and a new Diamond Jubilee Mark V Lincoln Continental. The bonus arrangement, plus his World Series share, gave Billy the distinction of being the highest-paid manager in baseball.

However well Martin felt about Gabe Paul's statement and the bonus, the Yankees didn't do too well in the first inning of the sixth game. An error following a walk, then a triple, and the Dodgers had two runs off Mike Torrez. But the Yanks tied it up in the second with a walk to Reggie and a home run by Chris Chambliss.

Reggie Smith put the Dodgers ahead again with a blast into the bleachers in the third, but Jackson powered one for all the bases, with Munson on, and the Yankees went ahead to stay in front.

It was the first of Reggie Jackson's homers in the game. In the fifth inning, he hit Elias Sosa for his second homer of the day. In the eighth, Reggie jumped into knuckle-baller Charley Hough's pitch and drove it some 475 feet into the center-field bleachers. No one but Babe Ruth had hit three home runs in a World Series before, and the Babe had done it twice; but nobody, nobody at all, had ever hit three home runs on three consecutive swings. It was an incredible performance, and there was Reggie taking his bows to the 56,407 screaming fans in Yankee Stadium, and Billy Martin looking on and applauding Jackson.

When pinch-hitter Al Lacey fouled out for the Dodgers in the ninth, the game was over. The Yankees had won their first World Series championship in fifteen years, and Billy the Kid had realized a lifelong dream.

"It's all over," said Billy. "This has been very rewarding. Now I can go home and collapse."

Back in the clubhouse, a thoroughly elated Reggie Jackson declaimed.

"Billy Martin," he said. "I love the man. I love Billy Martin. The man did a helluva job this year. There's nobody else I'd rather play for. Next year we're going to be tougher. We'll win because we have a manager who is a tough bastard and I'm a tough bastard. If you fuck with Billy Martin you're in trouble and if you fuck with Reggie Jackson you're in trouble."

Reggie was getting a car for being voted the Most Valuable Player of the Series. Billy promised Reggie he would be there for the ceremonies. Billy never showed up. The dissension in the ranks of the Yankees had not disappeared; they had been merely covered up.

"Don't believe everything you see," said Thurman Munson. "How could I ever love that son-of-a-bitch after what he said about me?"

After the second game of the World Series, Munson ran

into Gabe Paul in a steakhouse. Gabe asked him over to his table for a drink. Munson turned him down.

"I don't want to drink with you, Gabe," he said. "I love you but I won't play another year for Steinbrenner. And I won't play another year with that prick, Jackson."

Sparky Lyle wasn't happy working for Steinbrenner either, and had repeatedly asked to be traded.

Bucky Dent was unhappy.

Mickey Rivers insisted that he wanted to be traded.

And Billy Martin, toward the end of the year, on Reggie Jackson: "Off the record, he's a piece of shit."

CHAPTER TWENTY-FIVE

Losing

IN FEBRUARY OF 1978, GABE PAUL WAS NO LONGER THE president of the New York Yankees. He had moved West to assume the presidency of the Cleveland Indians, and George Steinbrenner found it necessary to appoint two men, Al Rosen and Cedric Tallis, to take his place. The absence of Gabe Paul was going to make a vital difference in the New York organization, and a critical difference for Billy Martin.

Far away from the hectic scene of the Yankee clubhouse, Gabe Paul, one of the wisest judges of talent in the baseball industry, as well as one of its sharpest traders, was of the opinion that Martin was the best possible manager for the New York aggregation.

"Billy's got a feel for them," he said, "and they've got a feel for him. I don't know exactly what it is, but Billy's got an intangible something that helps him stimulate the players, even those who hate him. Some people like to compare Billy with Leo Durocher, but for me, Durocher was much more tactically reckless. Their similarity is more off the field. Maybe the thing about Billy is that his lack of fear of the consequences rubs off on the players. He's always positive. In a slump, he's effervescent. He never had a defeatist thought."

With reference to the Kid and Steinbrenner, Gabe said, "They'll get along if they win."

The Yankees were going to miss Gabe Paul. Before he left the organization, he had allowed Mike Torrez, as a free agent, to slip to Boston. The Red Sox had bid more than the $1.5 million Gabe thought he was worth.

But before he left the Yankees, Gabe Paul acquired one of the great relief pitchers in baseball, Rich Gossage, for a con-

tract that totaled $2,748,000, including a bonus of $750,000.
And now the Yankees had the two finest relief pitchers in baseball in Gossage and Sparky Lyle. The Yankees would miss the
vast storehouse of baseball knowledge that Gabe Paul had
gathered in his fifty years as a baseball man, but Gabe felt that
he had to get out from under Steinbrenner's thumb. Steinbrenner, on the other hand, felt that Paul at sixty-seven was
getting too old for the frenetic pace of the Yankees.

Billy Martin was going to miss Gabe for his keen baseball
sense, his knowledge of nearly every player in the league. He
was going to miss him more because, ever since he had come
back to the Yankees as manager, it was Gabe Paul who had
been able to temper George Steinbrenner's ego for the good of
the club, his frequent tempestuous attacks on both his players
and manager, and it was Gabe who had managed to mediate
the fighting differences and the actual battles between Steinbrenner and Martin.

It was soon after Steinbrenner bought the controlling interest in the New York club in 1974 that Mike Burke, then president, resigned. Yankee manager Ralph Houk resigned. Lee
MacPhail, president and general manager, resigned, all in fairly
short order. Then followed other resignations: Bob Fishel, vice
president; his successor in office, Marty Appel; Joe Garagiola,
Jr., the club's attorney; and now Gabe Paul.

How long was Billy Martin going to last? He had already
been with the Yankees considerably longer than anyone had
expected.

In December 1977, a few weeks before Paul left the Yankee
organization, Steinbrenner named Al Rosen his executive vice
president. By the time spring training began, Rosen had become president. Al was born in Spartanburg, South Carolina.
In 1924, the Rosen family moved to Miami to help young Al
overcome a series of confining asthmatic attacks. The asthma
was so serious that Al often had to stop in the middle of a
game and would cough and gasp for breath. Fortunately, he
outgrew the illness and began to make a reputation for himself
as an all-around athlete at Florida Military Academy and the

University of Miami, where he starred in football and baseball and was captain of the Hurricanes' boxing team.

Al was seventeen when he broke into pro baseball with the Red Sox' Class D farm team at Danville, Virginia. Danville let him go, told him he'd never make a ballplayer. "Go home and buy yourself a lunch bucket," the Danville manager said. "In baseball either you've got it or you haven't. You haven't. Your reflexes are too slow."

That didn't faze tough, determined Al Rosen, and he promptly latched on with the Cleveland Indians' farm team at Thomasville, North Carolina. The Thomasville manager, Jimmy Greezdis, worked with the hard-nosed youngster and he made the team.

Al went into the Navy in the fall of 1942, joined the Navy V-12 program at the University of Miami, and became a small-boat pilot. He was on Okinawa on V-J Day and was discharged from the Navy in 1946 as a first lieutenant. Then he began his personal battle in baseball up through the minor leagues to the Cleveland Indians.

Ken Keltner was the Indians' star third baseman, while Rosen slammed his way up the minors: at Pittsfield in 1946, Oklahoma City in '47, Kansas City in '48, San Diego in '49. He was named the Texas League Player of the Year at Oklahoma City and the American Association's Rookie of the Year at Kansas City. The Indians brought Al up to the major leagues in 1947, in 1948 and again in 1949, but always there was the amazing Ken Keltner barring the way.

Finally, in 1950, the Indians released Keltner, who hadn't made a solid extra-base hit throughout the entire spring-training program.

That very first day Rosen donned a Cleveland uniform, he slugged out a home run and a double. The next day he repeated the slugging, with another homer and two doubles. And then went on to hit 37 homers and became the first rookie to lead the league in that department.

In 1953, Al Rosen slugged out 43 home runs, finished the year with a batting average of .336, and was named the Most

Valuable Player in the American League. And during a ten-
year period Al Rosen became one of baseball's hardest-hitting
third basemen.

George Steinbrenner, six years younger than Al Rosen, had
watched Al play, admired him, and the two Cleveland men became fast friends. When his playing days were over, Rosen became a stockbroker in Cleveland, and then a director of branch
offices for Caesar's Palace at Las Vegas, and when Steinbrenner formed a syndicate to purchase the Yankees, Al Rosen
became a limited partner. George felt that because Rosen had
played the game and understood the problems out on the playing field, he would have a better rapport with Billy Martin.
"It's not so easy," Steinbrenner said, "for Billy to face Al
Rosen and say 'What the hell do you know about baseball?,'
which he can do with me."

There were several heated arguments between Martin and
the new Yankee president, Al Rosen. On May 31, Thurman
Munson was forced out of a game against the Orioles because
his sore knees were aching and he could hardly move. Before
the game was over, Rosen announced to the press that the
Yankees were recalling a fast-moving young catcher, Mike
Heath, from their West Haven farm team.

Martin didn't know about this acquisition until a reporter
told him, and he was furious. But he was even angrier the next
day, when Rosen summoned Billy to his office to explain what
Billy meant in talking about pitcher Rawly Eastwick and
calling him "George's Boy," meaning that Steinbrenner had
made a deal for Eastwick and Billy wasn't sure what he could
do with the newcomer.

After the meeting with Rosen, Billy talked with sportswriters
before departing for Oakland with the team. "I'm just not
going to take any more harassment. I had it all last year.
That's enough. You call Rosen and tell him Billy wants it
known that Al Rosen and George Steinbrenner are running
the Yankees, not Billy Martin."

The next morning Rosen, after hearing Billy's angry statement, calmly said, "Billy Martin is the manager of this ball

club, he has been the manager, he will continue to be the manager."

Spring training for the Yanks in '78 was almost utopian compared with the turmoil and strife of the '77 season.

"I'm more relaxed this year," said Reggie Jackson, one of the principal actors in the '77 Yankees' soap opera. "We've been through a lot together. Maybe that's why we're working a little harder to understand each other."

Billy Martin said, "The players know each other this spring. Last spring they were strangers. It takes some time to know how to take kidding, to handle the natural agitation. It's like a marriage. When you are first married, you have trouble learning to live with each other. The longer you are married, the easier it gets. You have divorce in marriage and trades in baseball."

George Steinbrenner said, "We've built a strong organization and I'm leaving the running of the ball club to Al Rosen and Billy Martin."

So far so good. But the détente between Jackson and Martin was all surface and there was little substance to it. And nothing was ever going to keep Steinbrenner out of the Yankees' clubhouse. As for Billy Martin's analogy, he might have said more correctly, "You have divorce in marriage and firing in baseball." And the "firing" became a very distinct possibility very early into the '78 season.

April and May had been disastrous months for the Yankees, so far as George Steinbrenner was concerned. The "strong organization" the Yankees had put together was supposed to take off from the start of the season and leave the competition far behind; instead it was the Boston Red Sox who took off, and the Yanks were playing poorly.

In the first days of June, the Yankees dropped two to the Kansas City Royals, both in the ninth inning. An explosion in the ranks was overdue. It wasn't Jackson, as might have been expected, who took the brunt of Billy Martin's temper; it was Thurman Munson, and that by accident. The intended target was Mickey Rivers, but Thurman was in the wrong place at the wrong time. Mickey wasn't hustling the way Billy wanted to see him hustling, and the Yanks were losing.

"Hank Bauer, Yogi Berra, Mickey Mantle knew how to get a player to hustle," Billy shouted at Munson. "You're the team captain. Get on those guys who aren't hustling."

"I don't care about anyone else," said Thurman, "I play as hard as I can."

It wasn't exactly the response Billy wanted, and he went after Munson about team play, team spirit, and cooperation with the manager, and Thurman gave it right back to Billy.

The whole episode, which took place on a team plane trip from Kansas City to Chicago, and for which Billy later apologized to Munson, shook the morale of the Yankees and did the club no good, and it certainly did Martin no good. He was nervous, irritable, and worried sick. He had begun to drink seriously, evidently to escape his mounting tensions. The drinking wasn't going to do him any good, either.

On his way to Detroit for a four-game series with the Tigers, Martin grew bitter, angry, and quite depressed. Sitting next to a reporter friend on the plane, Billy said, "I give George Steinbrenner 100 per cent loyalty, and I expect it in return. If he doesn't think I'm doing the job right, he should call Al Rosen and tell him to do something. All this talk about me getting fired is disrupting my life. My son reads about it and it bothers him. My mother reads about it and it bothers her. It hurts my family and my friends, and it's hurting my health."

In the middle of June, the Yankees lost seven out of eight on a disastrous swing through the West. The rumor mills were now at work and sportswriters began to grind out stories about Billy's imminent dismissal as the Yankees' manager.

"I've been fired before," was Billy's reaction. "Last year they fired me five times."

But Billy was worried. Andy Messersmith, Catfish Hunter, Dick Tidrow, and Ed Figueroa were all plagued with injuries. Ken Holtzman and Rawly Eastwick had been traded. Sparky Lyle, still wanting to be traded, was less than efficient as a re-lief pitcher. Ken Clay and Jim Beattie were not living up to their promises. And the big guns of the Yankee attack—Jackson, Munson, Nettles, et al., weren't hitting.

Reggie Jackson had a word or two for the press.

"It's not Billy Martin's fault that we're not hitting. You go through periods like this. There's no doubt on this team, not with Graig Nettles or Chris Chambliss or Thurman Munson or Reggie Jackson. These guys know they're going to hit, and we're going to start winning."

But George Steinbrenner sang another tune.

"Why aren't our young pitchers coming along like other young pitchers?" he asked, rhetorically. "What's holding them back? Who's handling them wrong? I'll tell you one thing, I won't put up with this much longer. I won't stand for what I see now."

Billy's job was on the line, and he knew it.

"How can you take over a club, win a pennant in your first year, win a World Series in your second, and every time I turn around, I'm being fired?" he asked. "There are guys who manage for fifteen years and never finished higher than fourth, and you never read about them getting fired."

Logical, but meaningless as far as Steinbrenner was concerned, and Billy Martin knew that, too.

"No," continued the Kid, "I don't want to go someplace else. I want to stay here and bring in four or five pennants in a row. If they stick with you when you win, why can't they stick with you when you lose?

"I've got some pride, too. How do you think I feel about this damn thing? I don't quit now. I'm not a quitter. We just have to go a little harder, give it a little extra to turn this thing around. And we can do it."

On June 26, Martin and his agent, Doug Newton, met with George Steinbrenner and Al Rosen in the executive office at Yankee Stadium. Several days prior to this meeting Rosen told Martin that his pitching coach and longtime friend and confidant Art Fowler would be reassigned to work elsewhere in the Yankee farm system. Steinbrenner had been upset by the lack of progress shown by two of the Yankees' most promising young pitchers, Jim Beattie and Ken Clay; George felt that Fowler wasn't handling them—coaching them properly, and he wanted someone else to work with them. But some of the other players immediately saw this as an attempt to force Billy to quit. But at the end of a hectic two-hour meeting, a Martin who had been calmed down by Doug Newton not only saved his managerial life, but also saved Fowler's job.

There were other decisions that day; the most important was the decision to switch Reggie Jackson from right field to designated hitter. It was a decision that would have depressing results on Jackson and would be the move that would later prove to be a personal disaster for Billy Martin.

At the All-Star game break, on July 10, the Yankees continued their downward slide and were 11½ games behind the division-leading Red Sox. Billy had much, much to worry him.

Toward the end of July, the Chicago White Sox fired their manager, Bob Lemon. Immediately there was talk of Lemon replacing Billy as soon as Billy got the ax.

The end seemed inevitable.

There was an added item to the rumors. Billy Martin was sick, very sick.

Billy had grown wan and haggard-looking as the season progressed. He had lost nearly twenty pounds. He couldn't keep his food down, and he was drinking. He had suffered much of the season with a virus infection that he could not shake. In Minnesota, he almost blacked out before a game. At the time it was suggested that Martin enter a hospital for a series of tests. He refused, saying he didn't have the time.

"I've got a pennant to win. I owe it to Yankee fans all over the country."

George Steinbrenner had a proposition for Billy. Billy could resign for health reasons and George would extend his contract and retain him as a consultant for the New York club.

Billy wouldn't have it.

"I'm not a quitter."

He did see the doctors, however, and discovered that he had a "spot" on his liver.

The doctors advised Billy to quit drinking. Billy wouldn't do that, either. He wasn't going to give up his key to the private liquor cabinet in the Yankee clubhouse.

"As long as I've got this key," he said, "I'm all right." Meaning, "As long as I've got this key, I'm manager of the New York Yankees."

But Billy Martin's nerves were at razor edge. Something had to give and, ultimately, it was his hot and almost uncontrollable temper that triggered the inevitable climax to the Yankee drama.

As per Steinbrenner's request, Billy used Jackson as the cleanup hitter against the Kansas City Royals, but Reggie, who had been deeply depressed for several weeks and had performed poorly at bat and in the field, failed to hit in his first four times at bat. In the tenth inning, with the score tied, 5–5, Reggie came up to hit for the fifth time. Munson was on first base and nobody was out.

From his position in the Yankee dugout, Martin flashed a sacrifice sign, a bunt, to Dick Howser, the Yankees' third-base coach. Howser in turn relayed Martin's orders to the hitter with various hand motions and movements. And just before Al Hrabosky's first pitch to Reggie, Martin flashed the bunt sign. The Kansas City infielders, however, had seen that Reggie intended to bunt, and they moved in. Martin noticed the Royals' strategy and removed the bunt sign. But Jackson, ignoring his manager's orders, insisted that he would bunt.

Dick Howser called time and walked down the third-base line to Jackson. "Billy took the bunt sign off," Howser said. "He wants you to hit away."

"I'm going to bunt," Reggie said.

Reggie tried to bunt Hrabosky's second pitch and missed. He bunted the next pitch foul and then bunted the fourth pitch foul and was out.

Billy Martin was furious and Jackson returned to the bench ready for a fight. However, to his surprise, Billy stayed away from him. Instead, Martin walked over to Gene Michael, his first-base coach, and said, "Tell Reggie he can shower and go home. Roy White is the designated hitter."

The Yankees went on to lose the game in eleven innings, 9–7. After this game Reggie was still in the clubhouse and waiting for the inevitable confrontation with Billy.

Billy was absolutely livid. He marched into his office in the clubhouse and reporters could hear bottles being hurled against the wall. A couple of minutes later a clock radio came flying out of Billy's office and smashed against the outside corridor. Reporters jammed their way into Billy's office, stepping over broken bottles of beer. They confronted Billy, whose eyes were bloodshot, his entire body quivering with anger.

"No goddamn interview right now," Billy said.

Dick Howser, Cedric Tallis, and Mickey Morabito, the Yankees' PR man, walked into Billy's office and closed the door.

Meanwhile, at his locker in the clubhouse, Jackson was calmly undressing.

"I was just trying to advance the runner. I figured I'd get him over the best way I could," said Reggie. "I thought I'd be helping the ball club. Anyway, what the hell. If it was somebody else, there wouldn't be all this crap."

After a while, Billy stepped out of his office and faced a horde of sportswriters. "As of this moment," said Billy, still white and trembling with anger, "Reggie Jackson is suspended for five days without pay, effective immediately, for deliberately disregarding the manager's instructions during his time at bat in the tenth inning. There isn't going to be anybody who defies the management in any way. Nobody's bigger than the team. If he comes back again, he does exactly what I say, period."

In the next several days without Reggie Jackson, a calm, smiling, even joking Billy Martin led his Yankees to four consecutive victories as Figueroa, Ron Guidry, Jim Hunter, and Jim Beattie turned in four of the best-pitched games of the season as the Yankees beat Minnesota three straight times and then followed with a victory over the White Sox. But each night in Minnesota and in Chicago, Billy was asked about Reggie Jackson.

"I don't want any damn apologies," Billy said. "I just want him to get dressed, get out on the field, be in shape, and be ready to play ball."

In Chicago, on Saturday, before a game with the White Sox, Billy said, "I'll put Reggie into the game on Sunday. I hope he's done some hitting. If he hasn't hit in five or six days, I'm not going to stick him out on the field or as a designated hitter. It wouldn't be fair. He wouldn't be ready. I don't want to embarrass him."

On Sunday, when the Yankee team bus arrived at Comiskey Park, Billy went directly to his office and began to write out his lineup card for the game. He did not know whether Reggie had taken any batting practice during his five days of suspension, and did not wait to find out. He inserted Roy White's name as the designated hitter for the game and then complained about the noise that some fifty sportswriters, TV camermen, and assorted editors were making in the clubhouse. They were waiting for the return of Reggie Jackson.

Upon arriving, Reggie faced the cameras and sportswriters and started his soliloquy: "I did not regard my bunt attempt as an act of defiance. I didn't know it would get people so upset. If I had known the consequences would have this magnitude, I would rather have swung and struck out, and avoided this hassle. But the way I interpreted it, I don't think what I did was wrong."

Reggie did not play that day as Ed Figueroa pitched a marvelous game to beat the Chicago White Sox, 3–1. It was the Yankees' fifth straight victory—five straight without Jackson.

Fuming at Jackson's press conference and the continued talk that he, Jackson, wasn't at fault, did not apologize and did not take batting practice before the game, Martin exploded to Murray Chass of the New York *Times*, "We're winning without you, Reggie. We don't need any more of your crap. We don't need you coming in and making all those comments." Now he was beside himself and screaming. "If he doesn't shut his fucking mouth, he won't play, and I don't give a damn what George says. He can replace me right now if he doesn't like it. We got a good thing going and I don't want him with

his big mouth coming along and breaking it up. I don't want
to hear any more from him. It's like a guy getting out of jail,
saying I'm innocent after he killed somebody."

"After making certain that Billy wanted this conversation to
be on the record," said Chass, one of New York's leading
sportswriters, "I headed for the telephone and called my paper
to report this latest flare-up. I was talking with another reporter when Billy walked by."

"Did you get all that in the paper?" he asked.

"I assured him I had," said Chass. Billy couldn't contain
himself and he smiled grimly. Now the whole world would
know what kind of a guy Reggie Jackson was. A liar that you
couldn't believe for a minute.

"He's a born liar," said Martin as he and Chass walked toward the gate where the Yankees' flight to Kansas City was
boarding.

"The two of them deserve each other. One's a born liar, the
other's convicted."

The "liar" was Jackson, the "convicted" was George Steinbrenner. Steinbrenner was involved in an illegal political contribution in a Watergate-related case. He pleaded guilty, paid a
stiff fine, and was barred from actively participating in his baseball duties for a two-year period. The merest mention of the
case was enough to anger Steinbrenner. It was his Achilles heel
and a bitter pill for him to swallow.

George Steinbrenner had just arrived at his home in Tampa,
Florida, when the telephone rang at ten-thirty on Sunday
night. It was the first of numerous calls from Al Rosen and
from reporters all over the nation. Steinbrenner and Rosen
were appalled at Martin's remarks and were taking steps to fire
Billy.

The next morning, while Rosen was on his way to Kansas
City to get a firsthand report from Martin, the lobby of the
Crown Center Hotel was busy with reporters and ballplayers
with talk of Billy's remarks.

Upstairs in room 1138, Billy had not slept at all. He was
teary, red-eyed, and worried sick. He had several conversations

on the phone with his agent, Doug Newton, in New York. Newton had spoken with Steinbrenner in Tampa, and by noon Billy had decided to resign.

Some twelve hours after his infamous statements, Billy denied having made them. Nevertheless, accompanied by Al Rosen, who had just arrived, Cedric Tallis, and Mickey Morabito, Billy Martin, tearful and sobbing, read a prepared statement at a hastily called press conference in the lobby of the hotel, to announce that he was resigning as manager of the New York Yankees.

"I don't want to hurt this team's chances for the pennant with this undue publicity," he read.

His face was haggard. He wore dark glasses.

"The team has a shot at the pennant, and I hope they win it. I owe it to my health and my mental well-being to resign. At this time I'm also sorry about these things that were written about George Steinbrenner. He does not deserve them, nor did I say them. I've had my differences with George, but we've been able to resolve them. I would like to thank"—he started to cry—"the Yankees' management, the press, the news media, my coaches, my players, and most of all . . ."

The tears were flowing and it was becoming difficult for him to speak.

". . . the fans . . . for their undying support."

And quickly he turned and, with the arm of Bob Brown, a Kansas City friend, around his shoulder, walked away, the ex-manager of the New York Yankees.

"I did not ask Billy to resign and George Steinbrenner didn't ask him to resign," said Al Rosen.

Steinbrenner said, "The events that have transpired have little significance when compared to a man's concern for his well-being. These things, along with his family, are far more important than the game of baseball. I am grateful to Billy for his contributions as a manager of the Yankees. He brought us a championship and his apologies over this recent incident are accepted with no further comment necessary."

CHAPTER TWENTY-SIX

Back to the Yankees

THREE YEARS BEFORE HE RESIGNED AS MANAGER OF THE Yankees, Billy Martin had been introduced at a Yankee Old Timers' Day game at Yankee Stadium as the new manager of the Yankees replacing Bill Virdon and received a tumultuous welcome by the fans.

Now, five days after his sudden resignation, there was to be another Old Timers' Day at Yankee Stadium, and George Steinbrenner was busy planning an event that Yankee fans would never . . . ever forget.

Doug Newton, Martin's young, capable agent, was watching the Yankees play in Kansas City, after Billy's sudden exit from the team, when Steinbrenner paged him at the ball park and talked with him at length on the phone. Billy Martin, Steinbrenner suggested, should be managing the Yankees; and in the ensuing five days, Newton and Steinbrenner negotiated a deal by which Martin would once again assume command of the team for the 1980 season. There were more conversations, more discussions between Steinbrenner and Newton, with the result that Martin's contract was extended through the 1981 season.

Now at the Stadium for the Old Timers' Day game, the Yankee public-address announcer, Bob Sheppard, was at the microphone. He had introduced old-time Yankee greats such as Whitey Ford, Yogi Berra, Mickey Mantle, and Joe DiMaggio, and there was thunderous applause for all. And then, suddenly . . . a noticeable silence, and then Sheppard once again.

"Ladies and gentlemen, your attention please," began Sheppard. "The Yankees are pleased to announce today that manager Bob Lemon has agreed to a contract to continue as manager of the Yankees through the 1978 and 1979 seasons. . . ."

The more than forty-six thousand fans in the Stadium let go with a mighty torrent of "boos," interrupted only by shouts of "We want Billy!" "Bring back Billy!" "We want Martin!"

Sheppard pleaded for quiet.

"In 1980," he shouted into the mike, against the huge uproar, "Bob Lemon will become the general manager of the Yankees. . . ."

The crowd seemed hardly interested in that statement any more than they cared for the first. The booing grew louder . . . louder. . . .

"Your attention," begged Sheppard. "Your Attention, please. . . ."

The booing died down only because the throats were getting a bit hoarse.

"And the Yankees would like to announce at this time," shouted Sheppard, "introduce and announce at this time . . . introduce and announce at the same moment, that the manager for the 1980 season and hopefully for many years after that, will be No. 1: Billy Martin."

No one in the Stadium heard the rest of Sheppard's statement. No. 1 was Billy Martin, and the huge crowd went absolutely wild as Billy the Kid himself, in his Yankee uniform, with the No. 1 on his shirt, trotted out onto the field.

The noise in Yankee Stadium was deafening, everybody up on his feet, letting Billy Martin know how much they loved him. The cheers, the applause, the shouting went on and on and on. . . .

The thunderous cheers threatened to burst one's eardrums as Billy stood quietly on the field, next to his idol, Joe DiMaggio: Alongside Joe were Mickey Mantle, Whitey Ford, and Yogi Berra. Billy moved to Joe, hugged and embraced him, then Mickey and Whitey and Yogi as the crowd continued their incredible roar of delight. Five times Billy had to step out in front of the Yankee old-timers on the field and wave his cap to the fans as the ovation continued.

Finally, Billy walked across the field to the third-base side and extended his hand in a warm greeting to Bob Lemon. The two men shook hands warmly and embraced as photographers had a field day shooting pictures from every conceivable angle.

In the dugout, the Yankee players sat stunned and silent.

"I see it but I don't believe it," said Graig Nettles.

"Unbelievable," said Joe DiMaggio.

"P. T. Barnum was a piker compared to George Steinbrenner," said Phil Rizzuto.

George Steinbrenner certainly knew how to put on a show. But the baseball *cognoscenti*, questioning Steinbrenner's dramatic move, weren't quite sure whether it was no more than that, a dramatic move, a show, a publicity stunt; and there were many sportswriters and fans who doubted that old No. 1 would ever be out there again for the Yankees, urging his men to hustle, battling with the umpires, battling with the front office again, leading his team to the one place he had always wanted to occupy, No. 1.

In November of '78 Billy was involved in a tussle with Ray Hagar, a Reno sportswriter, in the bar of the Reno Centennial Coliseum. Hagar told one story, Billy Martin another. But it was Hagar who charged Billy Martin with assault. Billy said he was defending his friend, restauranteur Howard Wong.

The Reno affair, as the sportswriters saw it, was going to be Steinbrenner's way out of the promise he had made to Billy Martin and the fans. Certainly it was one of the reasons Billy Martin couldn't get the Yankee front office to sit down and finalize the terms of the contract that was to reinstate Billy as manager in 1980 and 1981.

Al Rosen said that part of that agreement between Billy and the New York club, in August 1978, was that Billy conduct himself "in the best interest of the Yankees."

Steinbrenner was more direct.

"If he's innocent of the Reno assault charges, then he's the manager. If he makes a settlement, then that's no good."

Wherever that left the fans, Billy was confident about returning to the Yankees.

"I have a verbal agreement with George. My word is my bond and I would like to believe that goes for others, too."

The young Martin and the old Martin are intrinsically the same. There is a code of honor that must be maintained: loyalty, trust, and a person's word.

Cynics will say, and with considerable justice, that it is something more than "his word" that motivates George Steinbrenner—the need, even more than Billy Martin's, to be No. 1.

And by the middle of June 1979, Bob Lemon's Yankees were in fourth place, some 8½ games behind the Eastern Division-leading Baltimore Orioles and fading rapidly. True, there were injuries to Rich Gossage, Ron Guidry, and Mickey Rivers, but more than the injuries, Steinbrenner saw the club play lackluster, uninspired, even stupid baseball. And seemingly Lemon could not develop the spirited leadership needed.

Bob Lemon had been a great pitching star for the Cleveland Indians from 1946 to 1958 and had won twenty or more games seven times during his years with the Indians. When he retired as an active player, he became one of the finest pitching coaches in baseball. Billy Martin selected Lemon as the Yankees' pitching coach in 1976, and the next year Bob became the manager of the Chicago White Sox. In 1977, Bob Lemon was named the American League Manager of the Year for his outstanding handling of the young White Sox team. However, the next year, owner Bill Veeck fired Lemon on June 30, 1978.

Hours after Veeck fired Lemon, Al Rosen phoned his good friend and former teammate: "Keep yourself available, Meat," Rosen told him. "Any day now, you're gonna be with the Yankee organization."

When Martin resigned under fire, Lemon was named to replace him. He took over a Yankee team riddled by injuries to key players and beset by psychological problems, and guided the Yankees to one of the most incredible comebacks in all of baseball history. Down by 11½ games at one period, the Yankees erased the tremendous deficit, won the division championship, the American League pennant, and then defeated the Dodgers to capture yet another World Series crown.

But that was in 1978. . . . And now in June of 1979, the calm, placid, easygoing Lemon Yankees were 11 games behind the division-leading Baltimore Orioles and seemingly going steadily downhill.

George Steinbrenner had to do something dramatic to change that situation. He had one clear option open to him. He had to bring back the one man with the well-earned reputation for turning losers into quick winners. He had to bring back Billy Martin, and he had to do it quickly.

Billy Martin had been on a scouting trip for the Yankees that took him to Anaheim, California; Boston; Toronto; and Cleveland. He had been scheduled to attend a San Diego Padres' Old Timers' night, then go to Iowa for a golf date, then head back East to Boston to scout the Red Sox.

But Saturday morning, June 16, Billy received an urgent phone call from the Yankees' general manager, Cedric Tallis. Tallis told Billy that Steinbrenner wanted to meet with him in Columbus and at once. Billy checked out of his hotel and flew to Columbus, where he met and talked with Steinbrenner for several hours.

"Billy," said Steinbrenner after an exhaustive session, "is this the time, or should I get an interim manager until next year?"

Steinbrenner knew Billy's answer before he put the question, but the Kid was not too hasty about his decision; he wanted some assurance for 1980 and 1981, and he got it.

Steinbrenner said it took six hours of conversation with Martin before he was convinced he was rehiring a "new" Billy Martin.

"Billy's changed," Steinbrenner said, "he's more mature. He's more solid. I'm not gonna say everything's gonna be hunky-dory, but the experience Billy went through last year has given him a measure of maturity."

The crucial moment in Steinbrenner's talks with Billy came on Sunday when the two were driving around Columbus and Martin brought up the Reggie Jackson problem on his own.

"We were just driving," Steinbrenner said, "and Billy looked over at me and all of a sudden he said, 'I got to get along with Reggie,' and I said, 'Yes, you do.'

"And then we drove for a couple more minutes," Stein-

brenner recalled, "and Billy looked at me again and said, 'You
know, we aren't gonna do this without Reggie. We got to have
him.'"

Finally Steinbrenner said, "I'm not putting you on the spot.
The job is yours in 1980 and '81, as I promised."

"I think we can do it," said Billy then. "I think we can turn
the team around and win."

And on July 18, just about a year after Martin's memorable
resignation, George Steinbrenner announced that, once again,
Billy the Kid Martin was the new manager of the New York
Yankees.

A crowd of fans breached the security area at La Guardia
Airport in their eagerness to welcome the Kid. There were
eighty reporters, broadcasters, and photographers to record the
return of Billy the Kid, their hero, clicking their cameras and
shooting questions at him from every angle.

"I'll give them [the Yankees] and their great fans my best
shot," he said. "I thank them for their confidence in me.
We've done it before and we'll do it again."

The Yankees that Billy Martin returned to were in disarray,
torn apart by injuries. They were mired in fourth place, 11
games behind the front-running Baltimore Orioles. Behind the
Red Sox and the Milwaukee Brewers.

The reasons were obvious; Ron Guidry, the finest pitcher in
baseball, had strained a back muscle and was out for a seven-
teen-day stretch. It was mid-season before he regained his winning touch. Goose Gossage, the best relief pitcher in baseball,
and big Cliff Johnson, the Yankees' utility catcher, got into a
locker-room brawl and the Goose came out of the fracas with a
torn ligament in his right thumb. The injury kept Gossage on
the sidelines the greater part of the year. Reggie Jackson was
counted on to carry the slugging burden of the club; he, too,
was injured and out of the lineup during the entire month of
June. Add to that injuries to center fielder Mickey Rivers and
pitcher Ed Figueroa and lackluster performances by Bucky
Dent and Chris Chambliss, and Billy Martin was soon juggling
his lineup like a magician to no avail.

But the biggest blow, the most catastrophic disaster of all, was the sudden tragic death of the Yankees' great star—the captain of the team, Thurman Munson, in a plane crash on August 1. Thurman was the team leader, the spark that often ignited late inning rallies to win the big games. He was the MVP in 1976 and had been the Yankees' star catcher for a ten-year period, beginning in 1969. Munson's tragic death cast a pall over the entire Yankee team for the remainder of the season.

With the demoralized Yankees faltering and 14½ games behind, the Baltimore Orioles romped off with the division championship and then won the American League flag by defeating Gene Autry's California Angels. The Orioles, however, were defeated in turn by the Pittsburgh Pirates in the World Series.

Then suddenly another shock that reverberated throughout baseball.

The calm and peaceful world of baseball was shattered on October 28, when George Steinbrenner fired his feisty manager, Billy Martin, for allegedly engaging in a fracas in Bloomington, Minnesota, with marshmallow salesman Joe Cooper.

Billy had just returned from South Dakota, where he had been on a hunting and fishing trip with his friend Howard Wong and had registered at the Hotel de France in Bloomington. Billy and Wong stopped into the bar for a couple of drinks, and at the bar Billy got into a rather heated discussion with Cooper. According to Billy, when the discussion began to heat up, he moved to the door and Cooper followed him, still arguing. Suddenly there was a commotion and Cooper was down and bleeding badly. He was taken to a hospital, patched up, and later said that Billy had sucker-punched him.

Yankee owner George Steinbrenner, apparently weary of Billy's misconduct off the field, fired Billy and replaced him with Dick Howser.

There will be another chapter in Billy Martin's baseball life. We are certain of that, for he is one of the shrewdest baseball

men extant. In another city—at another time—there will be
another team for Billy Martin.

It will not be easy for Billy, for he is a man not at peace
with himself or the rest of the world. And even the success
that he is driven toward cannot give him that peace. On a
number of occasions he has attempted to achieve a better rapport with his players, and the front office, but the shifting
sands of adversity and his own quivering emotions will continue to cause havoc within and around him. Inevitably there
will be the clashes with players, and with authority, feuds and
battles—and more dramatic victories before the ultimate victory or defeat.

The crystal ball is clouded at this moment in time and pre-
dictions come hard, but No. 1, the dynamic, tempestuous Kid,
who came out of the slums of West Berkeley to reach for the
"impossible star," found it, held it, lost it, is as confident as
ever. There is something about No. 1 that demands victory
above everything else, and Billy Martin is No. 1 to his fans, his
friends, and, most important, to Billy Martin himself. . . .